The BOOK of ME

A guide to scrapbooking about yourself

And the greatest of these is... love

I love my family and friends with my whole heart, and make every effort to let them know I love them, and value their presence and influence in my life.

by Angie Pedersen

with foreword by Joanna Campbell Slan

FOREWORD

Dedication. *To my children, James and Joanne, for providing endless reasons to scrapbook. To my husband David, for his unfailing support and encouragement of my dreams.*

Acknowledgements.
Heartfelt thanks and gratitude to Matt for babysitting David on countless nights with UT; Libby Weifenbach, Shimelle Laine, Toni Patton and Carol Hughes for their layouts and feedback on my rough drafts; to David Kellin for use of his prompts; all my layout contributors (see note on page 6); Elaine Floyd and Joanna Campbell Slan.

Cover credits. "Dreams" page is by Shimelle Laine; photo by Fred Murphy. Photo in "Strong" layout is by Roy Harrington.

First Edition. Printed and bound in the USA
06 05 04 03   5 4

Library of Congress Catalog Card Number: 2002190301

ISBN: 1-930500-08-4

Published by:
EFG, Inc.
St. Louis, MO
(314) 353-6100

Distributed to the trade markets by:
North Light Books
an imprint of F&W Publications, Inc.
4700 East Galbraith Road
Cincinnati, OH 45236
fax: (513) 531-4082
tel: (800) 289-0963

by Joanna Campbell Slan
*author of the **Scrapbook Storytelling** series*

I don't know about you, but sometimes when I look through my scrapbook pages I realize someone is missing… me.

When a pilot dies, the other pilots often fly over a funeral in what is called "the missing man" formation. They hold open the space where their comrade would have flown as a gesture of respect.

A similar hole appears in my memory books. You see, I take the photos, write the journaling, and save the memories. But frequently, I forget to tell my side of the story. I forget to ask, cajole and demand that my family take pictures of me. I get excited about the photos of our family outings and neglect to contemplate my inner world.

Angie Pedersen knows exactly what I mean. She's a Scrapbook Storyteller of the first order. She's learned to ask the questions necessary to identify the many roles she—and you and I—play in life.

I have only one regret—Angie's book wasn't around five years ago. Five years ago at a business luncheon a man sitting next to me said, "I've heard you are a scrapbooker." He went on to tell me about his wife who had been diagnosed with brain cancer. Her situation was hopeless. As her final weeks and days wound down, she found the strength for one task, creating a legacy album for their young sons.

To little boys of eighteen months and three years old, she would quickly become a faded image. She wanted them to know how much she loved them, and she wanted them to have a mother forever, even if she only existed in a picture album and in their memories. If she had had Angie's book, her task would have been much simpler.

I hope this foreword and this book compel you to start scrapbooking about yourself right away. Don't wait for a frightening episode in life to remind you we are mortal.

The woman dying of cancer knew exactly how best to spend her final days. You and I have a responsibility to create the same loving journal for our own families. Let's get to it…

Joanna Campbell Slan
Sunningdale, Berkshire
United Kingdom

Joanna Campbell Slan is the author of *Scrapbook Storytelling, One Minute Journaling, Quick & Easy Pages, Storytelling with Rubber Stamps* and *Adventures in Journaling*. Visit her online at www.scrapbookstorytelling.com.

CONTENTS:

WELCOME

Are You Missing in Scrapbook Action?

Experienced scrapbookers may see themselves in this scenario—you spend countless hours creating scrapbooks of your family, friends, children and pets. You showcase birthdays, vacations, trips to the park. Yet you are in very few of the photos because you are the one behind the camera.

Many scrapbookers shy away from creating pages about themselves because they don't have strong examples and guidance. *The Book of Me* is just the guide you need.

I was in the middle of a personal crisis. It was June 2000 and I had been a stay-at-home mom for several years. I was raising two beautiful children and running a modestly popular website. To most of my friends, I had it all together. But I lacked direction and a sense of identity.

I wondered what was special or distinct about me. I believed that anyone could do what I did and that I made no contribution of significance. Faced with this rather unflattering portrait, I set out to prove myself *wrong*.

I began working on a scrapbook about myself.

I wanted to show myself the gifts I had to offer and decided to showcase my life from the perspective of the different hats I wear in a day. I explored all of the pieces that make up my life—the sum of the parts that equal the whole person. I saw all that I accomplished

and all that I am grateful for. This special scrapbooking project allowed me to appreciate Me—the person I have struggled to become.

Your Book of Me

Realizing that other women may be facing a similar feeling or may be seeking ways to create a similar scrapbook, *The Book of Me* was born. In this book I'll guide you through creating your own scrapbook dedicated to documenting what you value most in life, what you've learned, the people you've loved and your hopes for the future.

You'll see examples of different roles people often play. For example, on any given day you may act as a mother, partner, sister, daughter, co-worker, dreamer or scrapbooker. Through questions and prompts you'll consider further the skills, values, people, experiences and memories for each role.

The Book of Me shows you how to highlight each of your roles by showcasing them in a scrapbook section. You'll see how to create scrapbook pages that honor experiences you associate with each role. You'll see how to combine

The Book of Me Title Page
by Angie Pedersen

This is the title page from my first Book of Me.

Supplies: Paper by K&Co. Font for title is CK Flair by Creating Keepsakes; font for subtitle is Joplin by Bright Ideas.

your written memories (or journaling) with photographs, memorabilia, quotations and other information from the Internet. Each section is illustrated by examples from my own scrapbook as well as scrapbook pages from other women to whom I've taught this process.

How to use this book

The Book of Me is different from other scrapbooking projects because it is about your personal memories, values and priorities. It is different from other journaling projects because it takes a big-picture perspective rather than working on the crisis of the moment and it incorporates mixed media—photos, memorabilia and quotations.

There are several ways you can use *The Book of Me*:

1. **Make one big book**. Work your way through this book, responding to the prompts you select from each section. You will have one scrapbook at the end of the project, all your stories in one large volume.

2. **Create theme books**. Use the ideas in this book as the basis for a series of shorter scrapbooks, each devoted to one aspect or role of your life. For example, theme albums would be Angie's Closest Friends; Angie—Wife of David; 25 Things to Do in My Lifetime. This format allows for a tighter, more defined focus for each scrapbook.

3. **Add yourself to family albums**. Use this book to spark ideas for individual pages in your ongoing family albums. The ideas presented here don't have to be a part of an album devoted only to your interests —pick out the ideas that appeal to you and do a layout here and there. The point of *The Book of Me* is to encourage you to make scrapbooking about yourself a priority. Your stories are just as important as your family's; make sure to include pages about yourself in your scrapbooking rotation.

4. **Design a remembrance album**. Use *The Book of Me* as an outline for a tribute album, answering the prompts based on another person's life. Consider using the memory prompts as a basis for an interview with that person, people who knew the person, or answer them based on your own knowledge.

You could split the role sections into separate scrapbooks, as suggested in the second option above. For example, you could create an album called My Mother's Friendships.

Turn the page and get started!

The Book of Me focuses on the positive contributions of your life, celebrating your gifts and blessings. It doesn't matter if you are married or not, have children or not, or even have scrapbooked before. Everyone fills different roles and they all deserve to be scrapbooked.

I hope that you enter into this practice of scrapbooking about yourself lovingly and with reverence—this is the ultimate self-care package. If you are in the midst of a struggle, it is my sincerest hope that this project will change how you look at your life. You were once a child of joy. You were once an adventurous young adult. You were once a new caretaker or mother. You are now a Woman of Character.

This book is for You!

Angie

Are You New to Scrapbooking?

Scrapbooks aren't just photo albums—what makes a scrapbook a complete memory is the journaling of the story and the inclusion of memorabilia.

These memories are preserved further by placing all elements in an environment that is photo-safe, acid-free, archival-quality.

This means using scrapbooks, pens, paper, adhesives and other supplies that are manufactured to be the safest possible for making memories last. For further resources, contact your local scrapbook store and see my website at www.scrapyourstories.com.

There is only one person who can write the story of your life, with all its foibles, follies, treasures and tears. That person is you.

—Kathleen Adams

1: CHILDHOOD

Definition of this role:
This section looks at the people, places, and events that shaped your life from birth through high school.

Your childhood is the basis of the person you are now. Your formative years directly influence your perspective and perceptions of today. Look back on that child you were and sing her praises.

What was special about that child? What did she love to do? How did her environment affect her? What choices did she have to make because of where, how and with whom she grew up? Describe her natural gifts and beauty.

It is important to note that we sometimes remember only the negative times in our childhood. Focus instead on the things that brought you joy and that formed a significant influence on who you are today. Remember the lessons you want to pass on to the special people in your life now.

In my scrapbook...
I called this section, "Angie as a Samuelson," because Samuelson was my maiden name. I wrote about my early school experiences, how my mom made me feel special and the music I listened to with my brother.

I also included a section on how participating in youth group influenced my high school years. I included my favorite photos of me at different ages to go with my journaling. Include whatever you think will help you illustrate the influential factors of your childhood—what about those years contributed to the person you are today? And on a lighter note, what makes you think of your childhood and SMILE?

Stage Clothes
by Libby Weifenbach

The dialog provides a priceless look into what kind of child Libby was. This "captured moment" portrait illustrates her at a specific moment in her life.

SUPPLIES: Pattern paper is by Memory Lane. Diecut is by Stamping Station. Lettering is Kiki template by Scrap Pagerz. Chalk is by Stampin' Up!. Font is CK Handprint by Creating Keepsakes.

AUTHOR'S NOTE:

Libby Weifenbach, whose page appears here, is one of 22 different scrapbookers who contributed to this book. You'll see the work of the others who graciously gave their permission to use their layouts in the coming chapters.

Prompts to trigger journaling

❑ Where did you go to elementary school?

❑ What was your hardest subject?

❑ What subject was the easiest for you? What (or who) motivated you to love that subject?

❑ Did you belong to any groups like scouts, church groups or sports teams? How long were you a member? Where did you meet? What did you do at activities? Who were your leaders? Who were your friends?

❑ How were you influenced by your high school years? What sort of things do you recall from being a teenager?

  o Fads or what was "hot"

  o Music you listened to

  o Youth group/church activities

  o Mentors or influential people

❑ Detail any memories of growing up with your siblings such memorable vacations.

❑ Ask a parent or sibling to write about a favorite memory of you (see the form, "What kind of child was I?" at www.scrapyourstories.com).

❑ How do you think your parents would describe you as a child? How would your sibling(s) and childhood friends describe you?

❑ What would your 16-year-old self tell your present self? What advice would your present self give your 16-year-old self?

❑ What could you see from your window in your childhood home?

❑ Complete this sentence: I am glad my parents taught me...

❑ Who were your favorite relatives?

❑ Talk about your birth—where, when, what events surrounded it.

I know not how I may seem to others, but to myself I am but a small child wandering upon the vast shores of knowledge, every now and then finding a small bright pebble to content myself with.

    —Plato

Children look at the world with their perfect little hearts.

    —Unknown

There is a garden in every childhood, an enchanted place where colors are brighter, the air softer, and the morning more fragrant than ever again.

    —Elizabeth Lawrence

Know what it is to be a child? It is to believe in love, to believe in loveliness, to believe in belief; it is to be so little that the elves can reach to whisper in your ear; it is to turn pumpkins into coaches, and mice into horses, and nothing into everything, for each child has its fairy godmother in its soul.

    —Unknown

As soon as I saw you, I knew an adventure was going to happen.

    —Winnie the Pooh

Children know the joy of living and are always willing to share it.

    —Unknown

Childhood Dreams *by Angie Pedersen*

This essay, written during an autobiography writing workshop, talks about my childhood dreams of a future career. The layout compares the essay to how my work history turned out. I didn't have many pictures of my years as a teacher, so I used a paper-piecing pattern to illustrate instead.

Supplies: Page topper is a bus cut out from Overall by EK Success. Letters are diecut from Fabric Brites paper by Keeping Memories Alive. Diecut letters are by Accu-Cut. Punches are circle punch by McGill and jumbo circle punch by Marvy. Font is Joplin by Bright Ideas. Paper-piecing pattern is from Two Peas in a Bucket, www.twopeasinabucket.com/pattern_shopping.asp

Keeping in touch with childhood memories keeps us believing in life's simplest pleasures like a rainy afternoon, a swingset, and a giant puddle to play in.
—Chrissy Ogden

I still live in and on the sunshine of my childhood.
—Christian Morgenstern

Heaven lies about us in our infancy.
—William Wordsworth

*I was born to catch dragons in their dens
And pick flowers
To tell tales and laugh away the morning
To drift and dream like a lazy stream
And walk barefoot across sunshine days.*
—James Cavanaugh

Sweet childish days that were as long as twenty days now.
—Wordsworth

Little girls, like butterflies, need no excuse.
—Robert Heinlein

To enjoy the flavor of life, take big bites.
—Robert Heinlein

Today you are you. That is truer than true!

There is no one alive who is you-er than you!
—Dr. Suess

❑ Were you first-born, middle child, the baby, or somewhere in between? What role did your birth order play in your family?

❑ What is your first memory?

❑ Talk about a favorite teacher.

❑ Describe your first love.

❑ How did your mother care for you when you were sick?

❑ What did you want to be when you grew up?

❑ What were your dreams? Did you dream of a big wedding or playing a professional sport?

❑ Write about your childhood friends—how did you spend time together? What did you talk about? What trouble did you get into?

❑ Do a page on recipes you remember from your mother or grandmother—what made them so special? How did it make you feel when she made it for you?

❑ If you were asked to share your wisdom with a child today, which life lesson would you teach? What do you wish someone had taught you?

❑ What is your mother's best trait? Worst? What traits of your mother's do you see in yourself?

❑ What is your father's best trait? Worst? What traits of his do you see in yourself?

❑ What did you do when you were a child that got you in the most trouble and how did your parents handle it?

❑ Did you have a favorite TV, radio, program as a child? Tell about it.

❑ Tell about the houses you lived in —addresses, phone numbers, etc.

Supposedly My Dad

Mama I know it hurts you
When you think of how it used to be
But you've more than made it up
To little sister and to me
Drinking made you leave the one
Who treated us so bad
But now you've moved away
From that man
Supposedly my dad

He may have a big house
That we never had
But that can never replace
What I have now, a real dad
I know he loves me very much
Though he corrects me when I'm bad
Still I wouldn't replace him for the man
Supposedly my dad

Written By: Elizabeth Wells, age 9-10

Supposedly My Dad
by Libby Weifenbach

Libby wrote this poem when she was about 9 years old. She kept the layout simple to keep the focus on her poignant words. It would be just as powerful to use a diary entry from your childhood, written in your childlike handwriting and filled with the emotion of the moment.

SUPPLIES: Vellum is by DMD Industries. Font is CK Penman by Creating Keepsakes.

- ❑ How did your mother spend her time?
- ❑ Were you responsible for chores? What were they? Which did you enjoy most and least?
- ❑ Have you ever stood up for what you believed, even when it was very hard? Describe the situation.
- ❑ What is your full name and who are you named after? Did you ever wish you could change it? What name would you have chosen?

Photo opportunities

- ❑ Photo of your house growing up.
- ❑ Photo of your elementary school.
- ❑ Photo of your high school.
- ❑ Photo of your childhood church.
- ❑ Photos of childhood friends.
- ❑ Photo of you in a scout uniform.
- ❑ Favorite miscellaneous photos of you as a child.

Ideas for memorabilia

- ❑ Color copy of curtains, quilt, or bedspread from your childhood room (use this as background paper for a layout).
- ❑ Photos, scans or color copies of academic awards and honors.
- ❑ Brochures from family vacation spots.
- ❑ Color copy of album covers of music you listened to.
- ❑ Color copy of sheet music you played in band or sang in choir.
- ❑ Scan or color copy of your favorite doll or stuffed animal.
- ❑ Recipes you loved as a child.
- ❑ Pocket page for grade cards or notes you passed in class.

WWW.

Pea Soup—quotes on childhood: search for "children", "childhood" or "child": twopeasinabucket.com/words.asp

Nostalgia Street—trivia, facts, and memorabilia from 1930-1989: www.nostalgiastreet.com

Fads of the 1920s: www.louisville.edu/~kprayb01/1920s-Society-2.html

Boomer Baby Memory Bank, for children born in the 40s, 50s and 60s: www.octanecreative.com/boomerbaby/index.html

Fads of the Super70s: www.super70s.com/Super70s/Culture/Fads/

Are you a child of the 80s? Find out here: www.80s.com/ChildrenOfTheEighties/

Fonts for kids (kid-like handwriting and other cute stuff): www.momscorner4kids.com/fonts/

Begin writing your auto-biography with these ideas and prompts: www.inspire2write.com/wordweav/lifelore/lifelo0.html

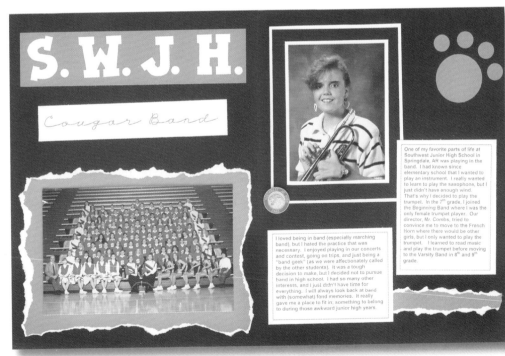

SWJH Cougar Band *by Libby Weifenbach*

This layout is strong because it incorporates bold school colors, gives a glimpse into the "big hair" of the time and includes an individual photo of Libby with her trumpet. In the journaling she talks about what she loved (and hated) about band and how it made her feel to be a member of the group.

SUPPLIES: Lettering is Blockhead template by Scrap Pagerz. Punches are circle punches by Family Treasures. Fonts are CK Cursive by Creating Keepsakes and Arial by Monotype.

2: CELEBRATIONS

Definition of this role:

This section includes memories that don't fit neatly into a role. They are the "slice-of-life" moments that contribute to a whole life.

One of the neat things about scrapbooking is the added insight of perspective—the instant analysis available after a period of time. After a time, you can draw conclusions and form clearer impressions of people and events. Recognize that what may have once seemed like a miscellaneous memory now is part of a cohesive whole.

For example, sometimes holiday memories, celebrations or traditions gain importance over time. Maybe you'll want to include a memory of something your family does every autumn. Say your family goes apple picking at an orchard every fall. How did that event change as you got older or included different people? Use your change in perspective to provide insight—how did you react differently during that event when you were five, as opposed to when you were 15? How was the apple picking different once you became an adult? How about after you became a parent? Do you continue the tradition today?

You can also use this section to highlight your relationships with extended family, like grandparents, aunts and uncles and close family friends. Did your uncle often joke with you— what did he say? What kinds of goodies did your grandma always have waiting for you when you visited? Did her loving preparation of your favorite cookies make you feel special? Do you strive to make your children feel that same bond with you? On a related note, what part did food play in other celebrations?

Caramel Corn

Dad used to make this every Friday night to take to the high school football game. It's awesome!

Ingredients:
3 quarts popped corn
1 1/2 cups peanuts (optional)
1 cup firmly packed brown sugar
1/2 cup butter or margarine
1/4 cup light corn syrup
1/2 tsp. salt
1/2 tsp. baking soda

Directions:
Place popped corn and peanuts in large brown paper bag and set aside. Combine everything else except soda in large bowl and microwave on high for 3-4 minutes, stirring after each minute, until mixture comes to a boil. Microwave 2 minutes more. Stir in soda. Pour over popped corn in bag. Close bag and shake well. Microwave 1 1/2 minutes, shake. Microwave 1 1/2 minutes, shake, and pour into large roasting pan. Cool and stir to separate kernels.

Karo

Mandarin Orange Salad

This recipe is so simple to make, but everyone always raves about it. Mom always makes this to take to church dinners.

Ingredients:
2 packages orange-pineapple jello
1 small can mandarin oranges
1 can crushed pineapple
1 container Cool Whip
2 boxes instant lemon pudding
3 cups milk

Directions:
Mix 1 cup boiling water and 1 cup cold water with jello. Add fruit and let set until jelled. Spread Cool Whip on top. Mix pudding with milk and spread on top. Make in a 9x13 dish.

Caramel Corn and **Mandarin Orange Salad** *by Kerri Sox*

Kerri's parents always made these recipes to take to potluck events. Her comments let us know why the recipes are important to her and why they merit a place in her scrapbook.

CARMEL CORN SUPPLIES: Pattern paper is Bitty Scrap Pads by ProvoCraft. Alphabet stickers are by Making Memories. Diecut is by Accu-Cut. Colored pencils are by Crayola. Font is CK Journaling from Creating Keepsakes.

MANDARIN ORANGE SALAD SUPPLIES: Cardstock is by Making Memories. Pattern paper is Bitty Scrap Pads by ProvoCraft. Stickers are by Frances Meyer. Diecut is Frame Ups by My Mind's Eye. Font is CK Journaling from Creating Keepsakes.

Miscellaneous memories of holidays, celebrations and traditions are important because they add to your rich personal history. They help form the traditions you choose for your family now. What about these memories is important to you? Why do you want to pass these traditions and memories on to those you love?

In my scrapbook...

I used this section to preserve the stories of my family's yearly visits to the apple orchard in September, my grandmother's from-scratch yeast rolls, and my favorite family vacation to Ledges National Park in Iowa. I scrapped several layouts about memories I associate with my in-law's lake house in Minnesota.

I also did a page on my most memorable birthday—I celebrated my 17th birthday with my youth group friends at the lake. The journaling on that page talks about how "at home" I felt with those friends, how deeply touched I was that they all wanted to help me celebrate my birthday, and how bittersweet it was, because it was the last time I would see these friends before I left for college.

Prompts to trigger journaling

❑ What day would you like to relive over and over?

❑ What were the best times in your life?

❑ What is one of the simple joys of Christmas (or any holiday) that you like to savor to the fullest? What was your favorite part as a child? How is that the same or different from today?

❑ Many people have a favorite holiday story or experience that they love to share. What's yours?

Sally, Kerah, Amy, David with Joanne, James & John (Angie is behind the camera)

The Pedersens!

James, 5½

S'more Family Fun

We go to the Lake in Minnesota every year for a week over the Fourth of July holiday. I love that my family has this trip to look forward to every year. The Pedersen's Lake house is such a retreat from suburban life. The kids really look forward to all that exploring time, and the intense bonding time with their grandparents. David & I look forward to relaxing by watching the lake as we drink our cocktails! The whole family enjoys making s'mores around the bonfire down by the lake.

S'more Family Fun
by Angie Pedersen

Is there a place you go every summer? Our annual trips to the lake are something we all anxiously await. My journaling talks about what each of us most looks forward to and the photos provide glimpses of how we spend our time there.

SUPPLIES: Background paper is Watercolor by ProvoCraft; Grass is by Hallmark. Stickers are by Me & My Big ideas. Title font is PixieFont by David Rakowski; journaling font is Tempus Sans by ITC.

HOW memory cuts away the years,
And how clean the picture comes
Of autumn days, brisk and busy;
Charged with keen sunshine.
And you, stirred with activity,
The spirit of those energetic days.

—Jean Starr Untermeyer

Oh Lord, make me a child again,
For one Sunday afternoon.
Let me sit at my mother's table,
On a summer's day in June.

Let me smell once more the sizzling roast,
Let me see it with my eye.
Let me taste again the sheer delight
Of Mom's homemade apple pie.

—Unknown

Grandparents are meant for kisses and hugs,
For watching rainbows and catching bugs.
For baking all of your favorite things,
For books to read and songs to sing.

—Unknown

Nobody can do for little children what grandparents do. Grandparents sort of sprinkle stardust over the lives of little children.

—Alex Haley

The simplest toy, one which even the youngest child can operate, is called a grandparent.

—Sam Levenson

Grandma's home is her grandchildren's second home, a sort of security blanket they can escape to when the world is unfriendly.

—Unknown

I don't think a really good pie can be made without a dozen or so children peeking over your shoulder as you stoop to look in at it every little while.

—John Gould

I am beginning to see that the things that really matter take place not in the board rooms, but in the kitchens of the world.

—Gary Sledge

Everything in life is somewhere else, and you get there in a car.

—EB White

Rest is not idleness, and to lie sometimes
on the grass on a summer day listening to the
murmur of water, or watching the clouds float
across the sky, is hardly a waste of time.

—John Lubbock

Summer is a treasure trove of magic moments.

—Unknown

❑ Describe the first time you remember saying "I love you" to someone outside of your family.

❑ Tell a favorite story about yourself.

❑ Talk about your grandparents—what are your favorite, treasured memories associated with them?

❑ What was your favorite family vacation? What was the worst?

❑ Describe your favorite birthday present.

❑ Describe your best birthday party.

❑ I will never forget …

❑ The most awful place I've ever been was…

❑ Create a layout on your extended family—how often did you see people outside of your nuclear family? Were you close to them, or was it awkward spending time with them? What did you love about seeing them? What was something you disliked?

❑ Explore the four seasons of your childhood:

   o Every spring, my family would…

   o Come summer, you'd find my family…

   o In the fall, my family went…

   o As soon as it was winter, my family…

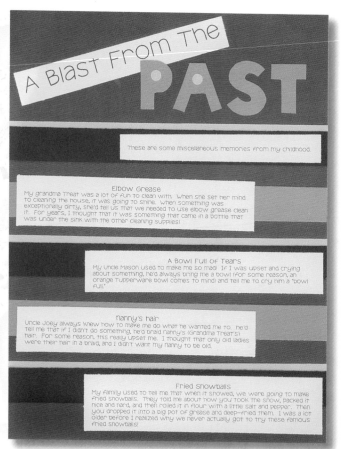

Blast From the Past
by Libby Weifenbach

Look Ma, no photos. This layout is packed full of memories—and is also a great way to use those paper scraps! Notice how Libby included four snippets of memories into a small space to provide a colorful "slice of Libby's life." Quick! What are four memories you could use to do this page?

SUPPLIES: Lettering template is ABC Tracers by EK Success. Font is LD Round by Lettering Delights.

Photo opportunities

- ❑ Photo of your grandparents' home.
- ❑ Photo of your grandmother's kitchen.
- ❑ Photo of a restaurant where you frequently celebrated.
- ❑ Photo of your family's frequent vacation destination.
- ❑ Photo of your extended family—aunts, uncles, special family friends—together at a celebration.
- ❑ Photo of you at the same age as an unrelated memory—for example, if you are journaling about a memory of your sixth birthday party but don't have a photo of the actual event, you can add another photo of yourself at age six.

Ideas for memorabilia

- ❑ Your grandmother's recipe cards, particularly for dishes she served at celebrations.
- ❑ Pocket page for birthday cards.
- ❑ Menus or business cards for restaurants where you celebrated.
- ❑ Pressed flowers from a special occasion.
- ❑ Memory Button of you telling about a favorite birthday memory.
- ❑ Ticket stubs from an annual outing your family makes (i.e. baseball season opener, or the Nutcracker Ballet).
- ❑ Small stones, shells or sand from trips to a lake in summer.
- ❑ Menu of items frequently served at family celebrations.

WWW.

Histories, descriptions and activity ideas for every holiday you can think of: www.holidays.net/

Recipes "like Grandma's Grandma used to make": www.freerecipe.org/

Homecooking, including a chart of measurement conversions for "heirloom" measurements like a peck, a dash, and a "slow" oven: homecooking.about.com/ library/weekly/aa041199.htm

Search for fun seasonal family activities at: www.familyfun.com/

Get tips on photographing in each of the seasons from the NY Institute of Photography: www.nyip.com (click on Photo Tips of the Month)

Monthly ideas on all sorts of different holidays available to scrappers: www.gracefulbee.com/ avenueb/photocorner/ index.html

Create a celebration journal for all the reasons you celebrate in a year: www.writersdigest.com/ journaling/articles/ 0601celebrate.html

Chocolate Gravy

by Libby Weifenbach

Do you have a recipe that, no matter how closely you stick to it, it never turns out as good as Grandma's? Libby illustrates why this recipe is special to her and how it is directly linked into memories of her grandmother.

SUPPLIES: Lettering template is Watermelon by Scrap Pagerz. Punches are Swirl Border punch by All Night Media and Circle punch by Family Treasures. Font is Scrap Caps.

3: YOUTH & COLLEGE

Definition of this role:

Take a second to center yourself on this time in your life—what stands out most to you about your life at ages 18 to 24?

For many people, the time between ages 18 and 24 was the first time on their own, whether as a college student or living in an apartment and working a full-time job. Remember what it was like to be that young, probably broke, and on your own? What was your life like? Consider how the choices you make in your early 20s affected your life path, whether that path included college or not.

One good way to help bring back memories is to listen to your favorite music of this time. What music did you listen to while you studied? What did you listen to at parties? What was playing in the background while you worked? Get out your tapes and CDs and bring on the memories.

In my scrapbook...

I called this section, "Angie as a Badger," in honor of my college's mascot. In this section, I talked about why I chose my college and my major, my friends and roommates, marching band, being a Big Buddy and the Badgers winning the Rose Bowl. These things illustrate what I loved most about being a Badger.

Indiana Chi-O *by Diane Adams*

Diane's journaling describes the family history of "sisterhood" in the Chi Omega sorority. The photos prove that you can go back and take photos today of places in your past! Also note the inked and chalked stone wall. You could also use this tag-title ideas for the letters of your university— like UCLA, UT, or KU, etc.

SUPPLIES: Tags, eyelets, chalks, jute and vellum. Font is from the Creative Lettering CD by Creating Keepsakes.

Prompts to trigger journaling

- ❑ Why did you choose your college?

- ❑ Why did you choose your major? Did it change along the way?

- ❑ What were your favorite classes? Who was your favorite instructor? Who was your least favorite? What was your "class from hell"?

- ❑ Did you go through rush? What was that like? How did that make you feel? Who did you meet during rush? Describe your feelings on bid day.

- ❑ Where did you live? Dorm? Off-campus housing? Sorority house? Who were your roommates?

- ❑ Name and describe your close friends at college.

- ❑ Did you meet your spouse/partner at college? What did you do on dates?

- ❑ Did you participate in any social clubs or activities? Describe the group(s), the meetings and the members.

- ❑ Did you have a job during college? Describe your work duties. Did you work your way through school, or was it just for a little extra spending money?

- ❑ How much did school cost (tuition, housing, textbooks, food, etc.)?

I would experience new emotions,
Submit to strange enchantments,
Bend to influences
Bizarre, exotic,
Fresh with burgeoning.
—Amy Lowell

Life is a fatal adventure. It can only have one end. So why not make it as far-ranging and free as possible?
—Alexander Eliot

O, what men dare do! what men may do! what men daily do, not knowing what they do!
—William Shakespeare

What will not woman, gentle woman dare,
When strong affection stirs her spirit up?
—Robert Southey

Youth, large, lusty, loving—
Youth, full of grace, force, fascination!
—Walt Whitman

Youth is wholly experimental.
—Robert Louis Stevenson

A school without football is in danger of deteriorating into a medieval study hall.
—Vince Lombardi

Rejoice, O young man, in thy youth.
—Ecclesiastes

One does not leave a convivial party before closing time.
—Winston Churchill

Angie as a Badger *by Angie Pedersen*

This is the title page to my section on my college years at the University of Wisconsin-Madison. The facing page includes journaling about my major and my roommates. The photos are of my dorm room and my first roommate.

SUPPLIES: Pattern paper is Fabric Brites by Keeping Memories Alive. Headline fonts are CK Flair and Wedding CD by Creating Keepsakes; journaling font is Joplin by Bright Ideas.

The good thing about being young is that you are not experienced enough to know you cannot possibly do the things you are doing.

—Unknown

We have a hunger of the mind which asks for knowledge of all around us, and the more we gain, the more is our desire; the more we see, the more we are capable of seeing.

—Maria Mitchell

I am not young enough to know everything.

—James Matthew Barrie

❑ What did you do to help you stay awake during late night study sessions? Did you listen to music? What kind of music? Did you have any particular foods or drinks?

❑ Where did you most often study? Did you study with others or alone?

❑ If you chose not to go to college, why did you make that choice?

❑ At what age did you leave home? Why did you decide to leave? Where did you live?

❑ Did you have a full-time job? What were your job duties? How much did you make?

❑ What did you do to relax, or in your time off?

❑ What was it like just starting out? How did it feel to be on your own?

❑ What lessons did you learn being on your own?

❑ What were your dreams and/or goals?

❑ What do you wish someone had told/taught you before you went out on your own?

❑ Did you ever feel like you missed an opportunity by not going to college? Do you have any regrets?

Wisconsin Marching Band
by Angie Pedersen

I wanted to capture the enthusiasm that comes from being a member of the University of Wisconsin Marching Band. My husband was a trumpet player in the band and many of our college friends were band members, too. I included lyrics to the school fight song along the borders and punched the punchies out of extra photos of the football spectators.

SUPPLIES: Punches are Spiral and Star by Family Treasures. Postcards from the UW Bookstore and diecuts traced from UW stationery. Victorian decorative ruler is by Creative Memories. Scissors are Deckle by Fiskars. Pens are Red Calligraphy by Zig and Black by Micron. Title font is Varsity by Brøderbund Software; journaling font is Garamond by Monotype.

Photo opportunities

❑ Photos of campus life.

❑ Photos of you with your roommate(s).

❑ Photos of off-campus housing.

❑ Photos of you at extra-curricular events.

❑ Photos of your favorite hangout —pizza place, pancake house, coffee shop.

❑ Photos of late night studying.

❑ Photos of your college mascot.

❑ Photos of what you did to relax or in your time off from studies or work.

Ideas for memorabilia

❑ Your school ID.

❑ Bill stub for tuition, textbooks or housing.

❑ Ticket stubs from athletic events.

❑ Pocket page for grade cards.

❑ Class transcript.

❑ Pocket page for school newspaper.

❑ Color copy of a food package.

❑ Color copy of page from your calendar or planner.

❑ Color copies of matchbooks from favorite hangouts.

I have tried to know absolutely nothing about a great many things, and I have succeeded fairly well.

—Peter Benchley

Of course we all have our limits, but how can you possibly find your boundaries unless you explore as far and as wide as you possibly can? I would rather fail in an attempt at something new and uncharted than safely succeed in a repeat of something I have done.

—A.E. Hotchner

Rose Bowl *by Angie Pedersen*

The most interesting thing about his page is that I had no photos of it to scrap! We didn't travel to Pasadena, we didn't take any pictures and none of our friends took any pictures. But we did watch the game on TV and celebrated the win as displaced Badgers in the Midwest. I wanted to commemerate the win with a layout so I had to dig up page elements from other sources. The photos came from an alumni mag-azine and I found an article at the Wisconsin State Journal website that offered a first-person account. The Frances Meyer football stickers even included a red and white letter jacket. You *can* create a layout with no photos of your own.

SUPPLIES: Paper is Red Gingham by Paper Patch; Football Gridiron by Oxmoor House. Sticker of Football and letter stickers by Frances Meyer; Rose by Mrs. Grossman's. Font is Arial by Monotype.

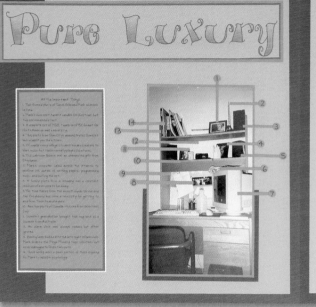

Pure Luxury *by Shimelle Laine*
This layout is striking because of its simplicity and color combinations. Note how the diagram of "all the important things" on her boyfriend's desk provides a slice-of-life. Even though this layout is not about Shimelle's own dorm room, she spent a lot of her college time here so it makes sense to be in her college section.

Supplies: Punch is by McGill. Pens are by Zig and EK Success. Colored pencils are by Prismacolor and Sanford. Lettering is Voluptuous from The Art of Creative Lettering by Becky Higgins. Font is CK Jot by Creating Keepsakes.

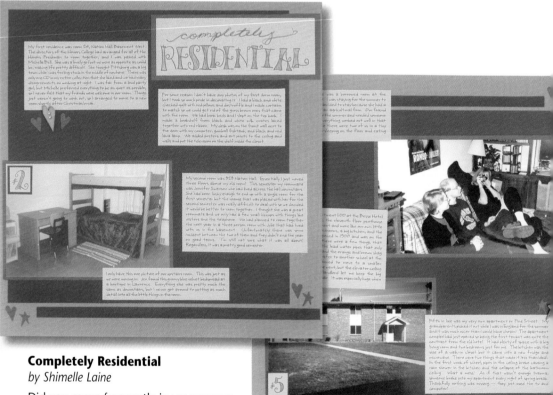

Completely Residential
by Shimelle Laine

Did you move frequently in your younger years? This layout documents five places that Shimelle lived in in just three years when she was at Pittsburg State University.

Supplies: Punches by PaperShapers and EK Success. Buttons by Dress It Up. Lettering is Concave from The Art of Creative Lettering by Becky Higgins. Font is CK Jot by Creating Keepsakes.

4. SOUL MATE

Your role in a committed relationship is one of the most intimate you will have. This is the person with whom you will be the most honest and share your most "true" self. While you probably want to reserve that special part just for that person, you might want to consider uncovering a glimpse of it for your Book of Me scrapbook.

Consider your role in your relationship and how you model the ideas of love, commitment, and partnership to your children. Are you teaching your children how to be a good partner in a healthy, committed relationship? By including a "soul mate" section in your Book of Me album, you will be defining all the lessons you want to pass on to your children about marriage, promises, love and cooperation. You will also be providing a place where your children can see what you love about your partner, reminding them that their parents' relationship is a strong, healthy one.

You may not be married, but still have a significant other. Or maybe you're between relationships right now. You can still include this section in your Book of Me album. Think of the times when you have been a soul mate, whether married or not.

Definition of this role:
This section looks at a committed relationship that has affected you and, perhaps, changed your perspective on life.

The "Why I Fell in Love with David" Page *by Angie Pedersen*

I had been scrapbooking for about six months, when I made this layout. (If I were doing this today, I would mat everything to make it stand out better.) However, this layout still communicates what I loved most about David when I married him. I color photocopied the drawing and the photo booth photos because they were already starting to yellow (not even eight years had passed).

Supplies: Patterned paper is by Keeping Memories Alive. Font is Mural Script by Digital Typeface Corporation.

Love: 1) Deep and ardent affection. 2) The condition of being closely tied to another by affection or faith. 3) A person who is much loved. 4) A strong, enthusiastic liking for something. 5) The passionate affection and desire felt by lovers for each other.

—Roget's II Thesaurus

Each time I look at you I'm limp as a glove and feeling like someone in love.

—Bjork

To the world you may be one person, but to one person you may be the world.

—Unknown

Consider how that committed relationship affected you, how it changed your perspective on life. Or if you have not yet found that person, think about what that person might be like. Dig deep for words to describe your ideal love, then tell how it is different from "real-life" love you have experienced.

In my scrapbook...

I wrote about what I love most about my husband, what my husband brings out in me, relationship lessons learned during marriage, and hopes and goals for our future as a married couple. I included photos of us while we were dating and some from vacations we have taken together.

Prompts to trigger journaling

☐ Make a list of dreams and goals for your life together.

☐ What do you love about your partner? You could write this in paragraph form or try making a Top Ten list.

☐ What does your partner bring out in you?

☐ What relationship lessons have you learned during your marriage or relationship?

☐ Include entry written by your partner:

o Use the "Tell me about Me" form at www.scrapyourstories.com/forms.htm.

o What does he or she love most about you?

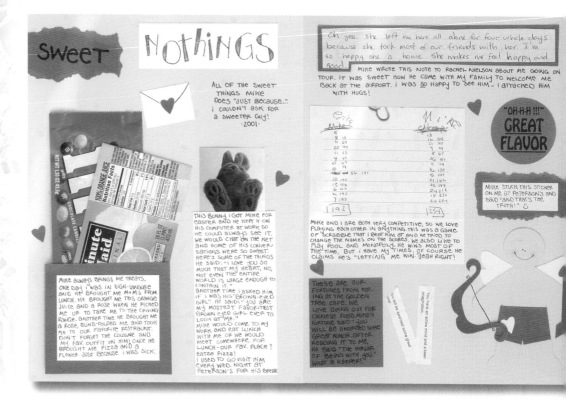

Sweet Nothings   *by Erica Shaw*

Real-life memorabilia shine in this layout. Notice the wrappers, labels, stickers, fortunes, notes and even game scores. Erica's journaling describes how these fit into her relationship and daily life.

SUPPLIES: Patterned paper is by Fiskars. Little hearts, envelope, and Cupid Paperkin are by EK Success. Pens are by Stampin' Up and Zig. Colored pencil is by Colorific.

o His or her favorite memory of you or time spent with you.

o The favorite gift you have given him or her.

o Have him or her complete this statement: I love it when she/he…

❑ How old were you when you first fell in love? Try to recapture the feeling with words and images. How did falling in love change you? How did it prepare you for your current relationship?

❑ Describe who you thought you would marry (your childhood fantasies). Now tell how your spouse is similar and different.

❑ What kind of spouse/girlfriend/significant other do you want to be? How is it different from reality?

❑ Write a letter to your spouse to be given on your 50th anniversary.

❑ When you die, what do you hope your husband will say about you?

❑ Describe "unconditional love." Is your emphasis on "unconditional" or "love"?

Photo opportunities

❑ Photos of your partner alone.

❑ Photos of you as a couple, pre-marriage or dating.

Love is not a matter of counting the years; it is making the years count.

—William Smith

The Eskimos had 52 names for snow because it was important to them; there ought to be as many for love.

—Margaret Atwood

May they never take each others' love for granted, but always experience that breathless wonder that exclaims, "Out of all this world, you have chosen me!"

—Unknown

To love another person is to see the face of God.

—Victor Hugo

The supreme happiness of life is the conviction that we are loved.

—Victor Hugo

I feel wonderful because I see The love light in your eyes. And the wonder of it all Is that you just don't realize how much I love you.

—Eric Clapton

And when the spark of youth someday surrenders, I will have your hand to see me through. The years may come and go, But there's one thing I know: Love is all there is when I'm with you.

—Christopher Curtis

Happy Together
by Angela Wilkinson

Angela created this layout to honor her 10-year marriage to her best friend. Her journaling describes their common interests and how much being married to him means to her. This man is her soul mate!

SUPPLIES: Patterned paper is k.p. kids by Paper Adventures. Frame is by My Mind's Eye. Fonts are Curlz by Monotype and Tempus Sans by ITC.

WWW.

How to say "I love you" in 69 different languages: love.welcome.ru/eng/view_one.htm

Romantic e-postcards with fill-in-the-blank love letters: passionup.com/letters/index2.htm

Valentine's font theme at FontParty: www.fontparty.com/valentines.php3

February 1999 at Ourvez! Police: www.multimania.com/clo/Police/fev99.htm
February 2001 at Ourvez! Police!: www.multimania.com/clo/Police/fev2001.htm

The meaning of giving different flowers: lovestories.com/romance/file.shtml?flowers

18 ideas for planning a special, romantic evening or afternoon (don't forget to take pictures): romance.lovingyou.com/encounters/

1000s of creative ideas and expert advice on love, dating and romance: www.theromantic.com/index.html

❑ Photos of you two on vacation.

❑ Photos of a kiss at midnight on New Year's Eve.

❑ Photos of you both at an anniversary dinner celebration.

❑ Photos of flowers he's given you.

Ideas for memorabilia

❑ A pocket page for love letters—from your courtship or a recent Valentine's Day.

❑ Menus from restaurants you frequented when you were dating.

❑ Pressed flowers from bouquets he gave you or from your wedding.

❑ Lyrics to "your song."

❑ Ticket stubs to movies you saw while dating.

❑ Time capsule information for the year you met and/or the year you got married (president, gas prices, city population, etc.).

❑ Use the forms in the Appendix to include journaling from your spouse or significant other. Get your spouse's input on their favorite memory from your courtship, why he fell in love with you and what he admires about you now. You can make a color copy of his answers (so you can have his handwriting in your scrapbook), or give him a photo-safe pen, and have him journal on acid-free paper.

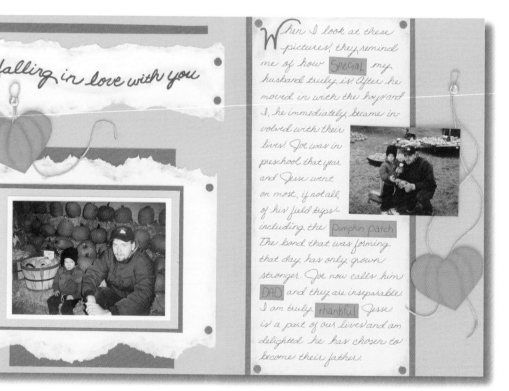

Falling in Love *by Jenni Omberg*
Your eyes are first caught by the clever chalking and little heart pumpkins. But it's the journaling that is really memorable. Jenni used this layout to communicate how grateful she is for the role her husband plays in her life, as well as the life of her sons. Scrapbooking is an effective way to communicate with those you love and who love you.

SUPPLIES: Brads, jute and chalking. Lettering is hand-drawn.

Jeff & Sarah *by Sarah Plinsky*

Not only did Sarah include what she loves about her husband, she got him to write about what he loves about her! Different perspectives always add interest to layouts. She also journaled about how their relationship started, their first date and their first kiss. The photos used span their 10 years together.

SUPPLIES: Paper is by Northern Spy. Lettering template is by ProvoCraft. Font is Arial by Monotype and CK Cursive by Creating Keepsakes.

About Us *by Shimelle Laine*

This layout follows Shimelle's relationship with her boyfriend from meeting online in 1996 to celebrating their fifth anniversary together. Note how she used miscellaneous photos that show the relationship's progression as well as the varied places they lived.

SUPPLIES: Paper by Autumn Leaves. Pens by Zig and EK Success. Lettering template is Block Upper and ABC Tracers by EK Success.

5: NURTURER

Definition of this role:

This section explores how you feel about yourself as a nurturer—to your biological children, adopted children, "furry children," or "rented" children of friends and family.

Most women have nurturing instincts. These instincts may be fulfilled by giving birth. However, there are other "mother figures" among us. These women adopt children to live in their homes. Perhaps they have pets and lavish the same love, money and attention on the animals that they would on a child. Perhaps they appoint themselves doting aunts and "rent" the children of friends and family, taking the children on fun afternoon excursions. Perhaps they become teachers.

It's up to each woman to see where this role fits. And once you've figured out how you nurture others, you can create layouts to honor this nurturing aspect of yourself. How do you take care of others? How do you love your children? What advice or life lessons do you want to pass on to them?

So many of our actions during the day are based on our role as nurturer. It is important to celebrate its very central focus in our lives, and pay grateful homage to all that motherhood has brought into our lives. By acknowledging what we value most about being a nurturer, we are reaffirming that our lives have meaning, and that what we do in a day matters. And by creating layouts about what you love most about being a mother, you also send the message to your children that they matter.

In my scrapbook...

I journaled about what I love most about each of my children, what I love about being a mom, what I have learned from motherhood, and a list of fun things we do together. I included photos of me with each child, a photo of me wearing a "PokéMom" T-shirt, and a photo of the three of us looking at a scrapbook I had made.

Dreams by Libby Weifenbach

The green, gold and black color combinations make this layout, well, dreamy. Read the letter that Libby writes to her daughter. Filled with her dreams for her daughter, the letter also communicates all that she loves about her own life.

SUPPLIES: Paper is by Colors By Design. Vellum is Parchlucent by Paper Adventures. Star punch is by Marvy. Pen is by Pentel. Font is Arial.

Prompts to trigger journaling

- What do you like best about each child?

- Complete this statement: I am proud of my children because…

- What do you like about being a mom?

- Make a list of "Fun Things We Do Together."

- What are your favorite books at story time?

- When you were a kid, did you ever think, "When I have kids, I will NEVER…._____." Have you stuck to this childhood vow or have you had to compromise? Do you see things differently now that you're a parent?

- What do you want for your children?

- Write a letter to each child, to be given upon:
  o Graduation
  o Their wedding day
  o The birth of their first child

- What recipes do you want to pass on to your children?

Photo opportunities

- Photo of you with each child (or of you pregnant).

- A good face shot of each child.

- A recent photo of you with your mom.

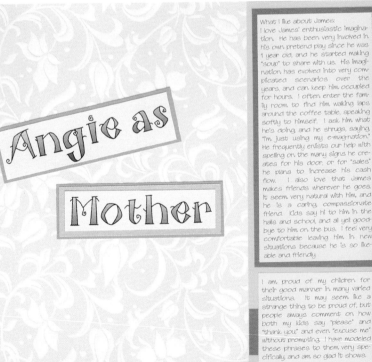

I loved you from the very start,
You stole my breath, embraced my heart.
Our life together has just begun
You're part of me my little one.

—Unknown

Before I was a Mom I didn't know the feeling of having my heart outside my body. I didn't know how special it could feel to feed a hungry baby. I didn't understand the bond between a Mother and her child. I didn't know that something so small could make me feel so important. I had never known the warmth, the joy, the heartache, the wonderment, or the satisfaction of being a Mom. I didn't know I was capable of feeling so much before I was a Mom.

—Unknown

Children know the joy of living, and are always ready to share it.

—Unknown

Angie as a Mother *by Angie Pedersen*

This layout talks about what I love most about each of my children along with what I'm most proud of. The photo of me pregnant shows all of the excitement we shared as a couple awaiting the birth of their first child.

SUPPLIES: Paper is by K&Co. Fonts are Joplin by Bright Ideas and CK Flair by Creating Keepsakes.

There is no other closeness in human life like the closeness between a mother and her baby... they are a few heartbeats away from being the same person.

—Unknown

- ❏ You common "mom" duties
  - o Carpool/driving the car
  - o Cooking dinner
  - o Giving baths
  - o Reading stories
  - o Helping with homework

Ideas for memorabilia

- ❏ Pocket page for Mother's Day cards.
- ❏ Pressed dandelion bouquets.
- ❏ Child's drawing of you (color copy the drawing or give them photo-safe markers to draw with).
- ❏ Encouraging notes you write to your child(ren).
- ❏ Ticket stubs from fun "Mom and Me" outings.
- ❏ Color copies or scans of favorite book covers from story times.
- ❏ Scan or color copy of positive pregnancy test.

Two Hearts *by Anne Heyen*

Little baby kisses are one of the best benefits of motherhood. You could use this title on a layout to showcase photos of you kissing your child(ren) and talk about how many interests you share or other cases of "it's in the genes." How have your lives and hearts combined as one? Note the color blocking with patterned paper and the striped mats behind the photos. I love the curly wire accents that go perfectly with the curly foil hearts.

SUPPLIES: Paper by ProvoCraft. Colluzzle by ProvoCraft. Font is CK Swirl by Creating Keepsakes.

Hugs & Kisses *by Anne Heyen*

Think of those special moments when it seems like it's only you and your child in the whole world. The color blocking, torn center for the wire flower and the popped up focal point photo create an attractive layout. Also note the chalking on the cut out lettering.

SUPPLIES: Paper by Debbie Mum. Wire is Artistic Wire. Dots by Pop Dots. Font is Diner by Sparky-Famous Fonts.

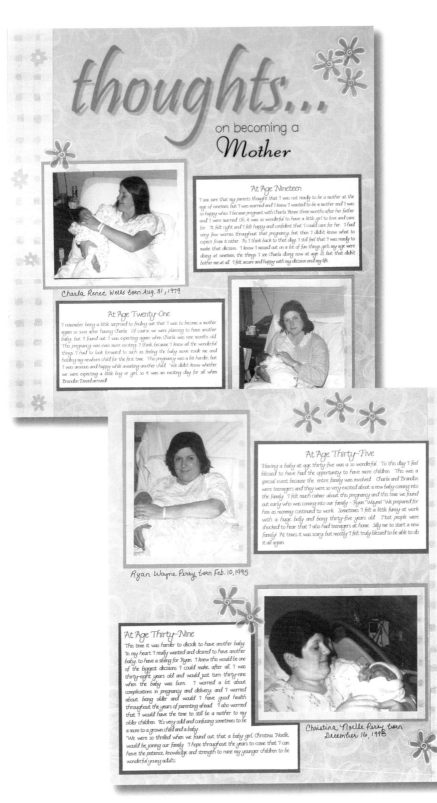

Thoughts on Becoming a Mother
by Bonnie Perry

Bonnie has had the unique experience to have given birth four times within a 20 year span! The journaling shares how her life and perspective changed over time. Note that Bonnie printed the page title onto vellum using the "landscape" paper orientation on her computer so it could be longer across. The vellum is thin so that you can still see the background paper pattern through it.

SUPPLIES: Paper by David Walker. Stamps by The Rubber Riot. Title fonts are Pristina, CK Primary and Liberate; journaling font is CK Italic by Creating Keepsakes.

A mother's arms are made of tenderness and children sleep soundly in them.
—Victor Hugo

Of all the rights of women, the greatest is to be a mother.
—Lin Yutang

Mighty is the force of the motherhood! It transforms all things by its vital heat.
—George Eliot

Mother is the name for God on the lips and in the hearts of children.
—William Makepeace Thackeray

The soul is healed by being with children.
—Fyodor Dostoevsky

Some of the advantages of motherhood: Endless wonder over rocks, ants, clouds, and warm cookies, glimpses of God every day, giggles under the covers every night, and more love than your heart can hold.
—Unknown

Every mother is a working mother.
—Mary Englebreit

Love isn't eternal; it's day to day. It brings home the bacon and fries it. It wipes noses. It makes the bed. Sometimes it even yells.
—Joseph Sobran

WWW.

Some general "mom-ing" websites:
www.momsonline.com/
myria.com/
www.momplanet.com/
www.gospelcom.net/
homebodies/

The Mom Files at One Scrappy Site:
www.onescrappysite.com/
homeorg/momfiles.htm

Microsoft Design Gallery of clipart (search for "mother"):
dgl.microsoft.com/

Mary Engelbreit coloring pages (her art is very "homey" to me):
www.maryengelbreit.com/
Workshop/
ColoringBook.htm

Coloring page for the Chinese letter character for "mother":
www.childbook.com/
images/coloring/
character-mother.jpg

How Much is That Doggy in the Window? *by Carol Hughes*

Much of Carol's mothering instincts are directed towards her furry children. Bogart is her firstborn. In the journaling, Carol tells how Bogart came into her life and how much he means to her.

Supplies: Paper by Over the Moon Press. Vellum by Paper Garden. Diecut lettering is 1.25 Block by Accu-Cut. Punch is Rectangle by Family Treasures. Chalk is by Craf-T Products. Tag and raffia are by Paper Refections. Eyelets are by Coffee Break Designs. Font is CK Print by Creating Keepsakes.

6: HOMEMAKER

We can't all be Martha Stewart or June Cleaver, nor should we even try to be. The gift of ourselves is the gift we give to our families.

Use this section in your Book of Me to record what unique spin you bring to the role of the modern homemaker. What tasks do you struggle with and what has made things easier? What dreams do you have for your home—how would you decorate if money were no object? What home improvement projects have you dreamed of and completed?

Create scrapbook pages on how you offer comfort and love to your friends and family. How have you decorated your most comforting rooms? What food do you serve that best demonstrates your love for the people in your home? How do you fill the needs that come from living with multiple people? How are you, and your home, a "soft place to land"?

By providing your home as a place to land, you let others know that warmth, security, and comfort is available when they need it.

In my scrapbook...

I opened my section on "Angie as Homemaker" with this quote by T.S. Eliot: "Home is where one starts from." I journaled about what that quote and being a homemaker means to me. I included a photo of my kitchen. On following pages, I added journaling blocks on "the home I'd like to create," and "I welcome friends and family into my home by…" I illustrated this journaling with photos of people enjoying food I've served,

Definition of this role:

In this role, you create and maintain your home—household chores, meals, family activity planning—everything that gets people where they need to go with clothes on their back, food in their bellies, and a sense of comfort that comes from a loving home.

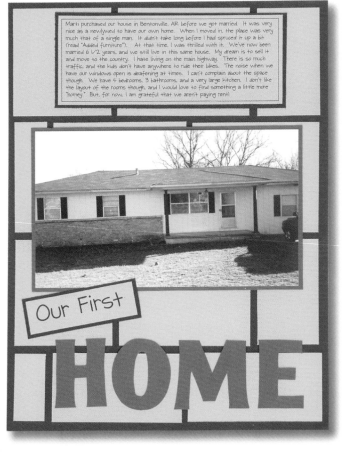

Marti purchased our house in Bentonville, AR before we got married. It was very nice as a newlywed to have our own home. When I moved in, the place was very much that of a single man. It didn't take long before I had spruced it up a bit (read "Added furniture"). At that time, I was thrilled with it. We've now been married 6 1/2 years, and we still live in this same house. My dream is to sell it and move to the country. I hate living on the main highway. There is so much traffic, and the kids don't have anywhere to ride their bikes. The noise when we have our windows open is deafening at times. I can't complain about the space though. We have 4 bedrooms, 3 bathrooms, and a very large kitchen. I don't like the layout of the rooms though, and I would love to find something a little more "homey." But, for now, I am grateful that we aren't paying rent!

Our First HOME

Our First Home
by Libby Weifenbach

This is the perfect ode to a first home. It includes a good, clear picture of the front of the house and is accompanied by journaling describing what Libby loves and hates about the house. She also talks about how she turned this bachelor pad into a family home.

Supplies: Lettering template is Kiki by Scrap Pagerz. Font is CK Journaling by Creating Keepsakes.

Where we love is home ...home that our feet may leave, but not our hearts.
—Oliver Wendell Holmes

Home is where one starts from.
—T.S. Eliot

It takes a heap o'living in a house to make it home.
—Edgar Albert Guest

What is more agreeable than one's home?
—Cicero

and parties I've planned. I also included a layout that described how I have struggled with finding an orderly way to maintain my home and what I have found to work best for me.

Prompts to trigger journaling

❑ What has helped you get a handle on housework, or what do you find hardest about managing a home?

❑ Complete this phrase: The home I'd like to create is…

❑ What do you do to welcome friends and family to your home? What preparations do you make? What food do you serve?

❑ How does the way you have decorated reflect on you? What do your decorating decisions and style say about you? How would you change things?

❑ How have you made your house a home?

❑ Virginia Woolf writes about the importance of having a "Room of One's Own." How would you decorate this room all for your own? What would you do in it?

Photo opportunities

❑ Photo of your home in each of the four seasons (consider making this a mosaic page).

❑ Photo of you in the kitchen.

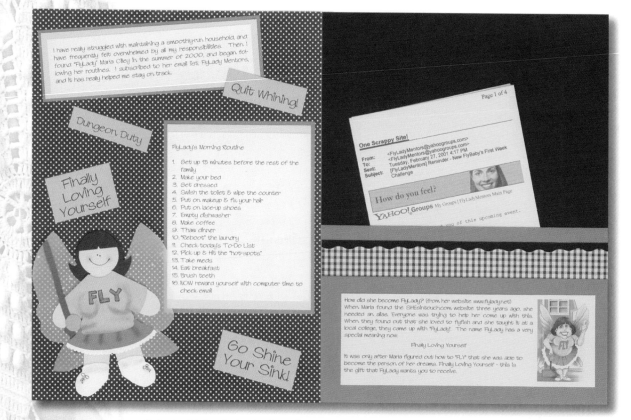

Ode to FlyLady *by Angie Pedersen*

Do you have a mentor or author to thank? This layout honors the struggle I have had with maintaining a smoothly-run household and how FlyLady Marla Cilley helped me through her website, www.flylady.net. I printed out the Morning Routine and Fly-Lady history from the site along with one of her e-mail reminders that I included in the pocket page on the right.

SUPPLIES: Paper by Paper Patch. Paper doll is Paperkins by EK Success. Font is Joplin by Bright Ideas.

- ❑ Photo of your "lived-in" family room.
- ❑ Photo of you with family planner or making grocery list.
- ❑ Photo of people enjoying a festive meal you've planned and prepared.

Ideas for memorabilia

- ❑ Paint chips, wallpaper and upholstery samples decorating a room you've dreamed of (completed or not)—"the home I'd like to create..."
- ❑ Grocery lists and receipts—particularly for a dinner party.
- ❑ Copy of a family calendar, with people going in every direction.
- ❑ Recipe page for your favorite comfort food or your favorite "impress-the-guests" dish.
- ❑ Pocket page for thank you notes from people appreciating your hospitality.

Home, the spot of earth supremely blest a dearer, sweeter spot than all the rest.

—Robert Montgomery

So much of what we learn of love we learn at home.

—Unknown

May its doors be open to those in need, and its rooms be filled with kindness. May joy shine from its windows. And His presence never leave it.

—a Jewish home blessing

Dining Room *by Lisa Schmitt*

The decision-making of home decorating makes a great story. Lisa used a piece of the wallpaper to make a pocket which holds sketches of furniture pieces, Polaroids and a list of the pieces were purchased.

SUPPLIES: Embossed paper is by K&Co. Cardstock is by Bazzill Basics. Stickers are by David Walker for Colorbok. Eyelets are by Impress. Pen is by Sakura. Colored pencils are by Lyra Rembrandt.

WWW.

Home management articles and tips at One Scrappy Site: www.onescrappysite.com/homeo.htm

FlyLady, my personal role model for home management: www.flylady.net

Discovery Channel's Home Matters TV show: dsc.discovery.com/fansites/homematters/homematters.html

The Learning Channel's Trading Spaces decorating TV show: tlc.discovery.com/fansites/tradingspaces/tradingspaces.html

Organize, declutter, and simplify with OrganizedHome.com (be sure to take before and after pictures): www.organizedhome.com/

Entertaining at About.com (take pictures of any party you host): entertaining.about.com/index.htm

The home I'd like to create has a bed and clean linens ready for visitors, tasty good to serve family and friends, and comfortable furniture to sit on for chatting. I want my family and guests to feel comfortable in the knowledge that all details have been taken care of so time spent visiting is relaxed. I want my home to be a place where people feel welcome, comfortable, relaxed, and loved.

I love entertaining in my home! I welcome friends & family by planning yummy appetizers, snacks, and filling meals; by looking them in the eye while talking, and letting them know how glad I am to be in their company.

Entertaining at Home *by Angie Pedersen*
This layout talks about what kind of home I want to share with my family and guests. It includes photos of people enjoying themselves at parties I've planned.

Supplies: Paper is Swiss Dot by Paper Patch and Green Plaids by Keeping Memories Alive. Font is Joplin by Bright Ideas. Torn posies border idea is from the shared files of the MEScrappers mailing list: http://groups.yahoo.com/group/MEScrappers.

7: FRIENDSHIP

Definition of this role: In this section of your Book of Me, you'll explore your relationships with your closest friends.

Oprah Winfrey describes friendship in her opening essay in the August 2001 issue of *O Magazine*. "I wouldn't be who I am without my friends, many of whom I work with, create with, and bond with daily. I rely on them to tell me the truth. To keep me grounded. To keep this big life I live in perspective. My friends are my therapy, my release, my sounding board—my safe harbor."

According to Aristotle, friendship is "the mutual love of people who wish each other well." Who fits this description in your life? Where do you fit this description? To whom are you "intimately attached"? Think about:

❑ How and when you met?

❑ What drew you to them?

❑ What you admire about them?

❑ What you have learned from them?

❑ What each of your friends has added to the person you are now?

❑ What kind of friend are you to them?

It is with your friends that you are the most yourself. You share with them your innermost thoughts, concerns and dreams. Your friends know who you are and help you imagine the person you might become, and

Toni *by Libby Weifenbach*

Toni's name is showcased with the use of tags, complete with little paper ties at the top. The journaling gives an intimate look at the history of their friendship and describes how they fixed their "catty" verbal exchanges.

Supplies: Tag is by Stampendous. Letter template is CurlyQ by Scrap Pagerz. Font is LD Diary by Lettering Delights

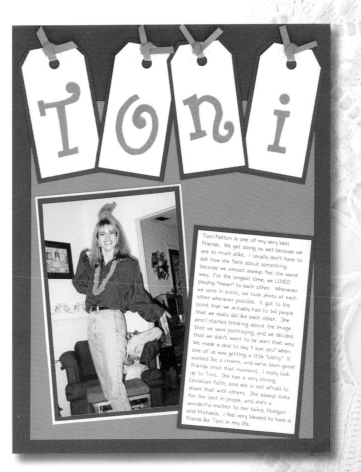

love you through the process. You celebrate with your friends all that is going right in your life and hold hands with them to wade through the tough times. Each of your friendships may illustrate a different facet of yourself and help complete your self-portrait.

In my scrapbook...

I looked back over my life and picked out the friendships that have made the most significant impacts on who I am, choosing friends from high school, college and more recent times. I journaled about how we met, what we did when we were together, what I admire most about each of them, and what I have learned from them. I included photos of me with each friend.

I want to note that I included a page describing my friendship with a woman I no longer see. It was not an easy layout to do, but therapeutic. I wrote about all of the points I listed above, then added how the relationship ended, and what I miss most about her. I used "hidden journaling" to tell the more painful parts of the story, to protect it from casual viewers of my scrapbook, while still preserving the memory. See the included example for an explanation of how this works.

Prompts to trigger journaling

❑ Where and how did you meet?

❑ What do you do (or did you do) with your friends?

❑ What do you admire about them?

❑ What have you learned from your friends?

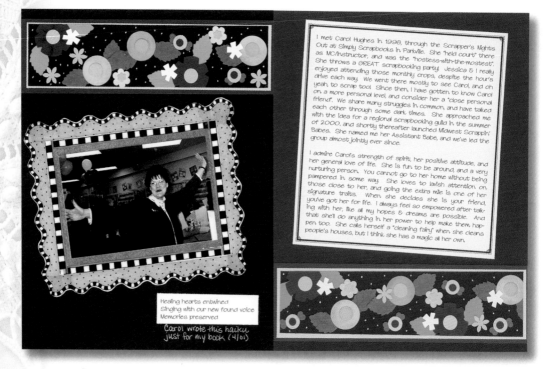

Ode to Carol *by Angie Pedersen*
What friend would you like to write an "ode" to? This layout is made even more special with the haiku poem written by Carol. The punchart is inspired by art from Mary Engelbreit.

SUPPLIES: Paper by ProvoCraft. Stickers are by Me & My Big Ideas. Circle punches are by Marvy; Daisy and Pom PaperShapers by EK Success; Birch Leaf and 6-Petal Flowers by Family Treasures. Chalk by Craf-T Products. Border clipart by MS-Publisher. Font is Joplin by Bright Ideas.

- What do your friends like about you?
- How is your life impacting your friends' lives?
- What qualities do you see in your friends that you would like to include in your life?
- List 10 people who have help shape who you are today, either positively or negatively
- Include "testimonials" written by friends
  - Favorite things about you.
  - First and current impressions of you.
  - What have they learned from you?
  - What do they admire about you?

Photo opportunities

- Photos of you with each of your close friends.
- Photo of you, and one of your friend, at around the same age that you met.
- Photo of cars you drove at the time, particularly if you spent a lot of time in the car together.
- Photo of restaurants you liked to go to.
- Photo of school(s) you attended together.
- Photo of the dorm room or apartment you shared.
- Photos of movie and music stars you swooned over.

She is a friend of my mind. She gather me, man. The pieces I am, she gather them and give them back to me in all the right order. It's good, you know, when you got a woman who is a friend of your mind.

—Toni Morrison

A friend is a second self.

—Aristotle

And in the sweetness of friendship let there be laughter, and sharing of pleasures. For in the dew of little things the heart finds its morning and is refreshed.

—Kahlil Gibran

The shared memories brought smiles, laughter, a few tears and, at last, a sense of contentment. For slowly, from our treasured memories a kindred bond began to emerge.

That's how it is with people sometimes. When you least expect it, a common thread—golden, at that—begins to weave together the fabric of friendship.

—Mary Kay Shanley

True friendship comes when silence between two people is comfortable.

—David Gentry

A true friend is someone who thinks that you are a good egg even though he knows that you are slightly cracked.

—Bernard Meltzer

left: Abby + Shannon "zerbet" Angie at her H.S. graduation

below: Wendy's restaurant where Shannon + I frequently bought Frosty malts

may 1989

above: Shannon's former house

right: Shannon demonstrates her singular talent of hanging a spoon on her nose - art Institute 1987

Memories of a Toyota Camry

A dark gleaming machine races down the street, stereo blasting, windows down, two cool chicks in sunglasses in the front seat. The car screeches around the corner. The two girls laugh hysterically at the Frosty malt which is now on one of the girls' noses, mine. This car is my favorite place, and it's not even mine. It belongs to my best friend, Shannon. This mean, little dark brown 1983 Toyota Camry holds many good memories for me, memories of sight, sound, and touch, memories of conversations, and lastly, memories of the places we've been.

When I think of Shannon's car, I can almost see, feel, and hear the car itself. I can see the light brown corduroy interior. I can see the green and gold Shawnee Mission South graduation tassle hanging from the rearview mirror. I can see the cinnamon - sugar spread on the dashboard and console from a slight mishap at Taco Bell. I can feel the music drumming into my fingers through the dashboard. I can feel the wind on my face and arm through the open window. I can hear music from tapes, 101 KCFX, movie soundtracks. I

My sophomore Honors English teacher gave us an assignment to write a five-paragraph theme on our favorite place. I chose Shannon's Toyota Camry car. I got a perfect score on my paper.

THEME ASSIGNMENT: Write a five-paragraph theme about a place. Due first of class on Tues, April 14

Follow the standard expository theme form. Although the form is expository, you will need to use descriptive techniques as well. (Use anecdotes, too, if they are useful.) Try to use as many appeals to the five senses as possible—evoking images of the place rather than explaining about it. If the place is not local, look at pictures of it, if they are available, to help you recall images. In fact, I would welcome the pictures with your theme. Samples of the themes and pictures will be placed on the bulletin board.

Ode to Shannon *by Angie Pedersen*

While I had pictures of my friend Shannon from high school, I went back and took pictures of the monuments. The pictures of Shannon are over 10 years old but the monument photos are circa 2001! If you don't have pictures of special places, go back and take them now or e-mail a friend who's closer by and ask them to take them for you.

SUPPLIES: Paper is by Color By Design.

Ideas for memorabilia

- ☐ Pocket page for notes from friends.
- ☐ Ticket stubs for movies you saw together.
- ☐ Menus from restaurants you frequented.
- ☐ Recipe of cookies you made together on weekends.

Ally *by Angie Pedersen*

The use of "hidden journaling" allows you to cover personal stories. It's also useful for layouts that incorporate greeting cards. Cindy Bradley of San Bernadino, CA, taught me this method. Place the layout in the page protector, then use an Exacto knife to carefully cut a little flap around the area you want to open. Use Pioneer Photo Memory Mounting Tape double-sided tape. It's clear and doesn't show through the page protector. Use the tape to line the area of the memorabilia underneath the open page protector flap. Peel off the protective tape liner and adhere the protector to the memorabilia. You won't be able to remove the layout from the protector after this, but you can open the protector to see the contents inside.

Supplies: Brads, jute and chalking. Lettering is hand-drawn.

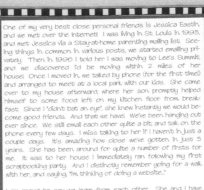

(left)
ice skating with her family ~ 12/00

(below)
after Liz's wedding ~ 8/20/00

One of my very best close personal friends is Jessica Eastin, and we met over the Internet! I was living in St. Louis in 1995, and met Jessica via a Stay-at-home parenting mailing list. Seeing things in common in various posts, we started emailing privately. Then in 1996 I told her I was moving to Lee's Summit, and we discovered I'd be moving within 2 miles of her house! Once I moved in, we talked by phone (for the first time!) and arranged to meet at a local park with our kids. She came over to my house afterward, where her son promptly helped himself to some food left on my kitchen floor from breakfast. Since I 'didn't bat an eye', she knew instantly we would become good friends. And that we have! We've been hanging out ever since. We still email each other quite a bit, and talk on the phone every few days. I miss talking to her if I haven't in just a couple days. It's amazing how close we've gotten. In just 5 years. She has been around for quite a number of firsts for me. It was to her house I immediately ran following my first scrapbooking party. And I distinctly remember going for a walk with her, and saying, 'I'm thinking of doing a website.'

I am proud to say we learn from each other. She and I have had countless conversations on how best to manage our households, and we are both on FlyLady's mailing list. We discuss parenting issues, as well as our newly acquired scrapbooking tools & techniques. I can also call Jessica with any pharmacy question I have, and there have been many! Like when Joanne hit her front tooth on the bathtub, I called Jessica frantically 'Which do I give her, Tylenol or Advil???' (Answer: either)

Jessica is just the best, a true friend. She has sent me notes in the mail when I'm having a hard time, or to congratulate me on my website's mention in Creating Keepsakes. She calls because she misses talking to me. She is a very sympathetic listener, and easy to talk to. I have learned the value & meaning of a solid friendship from her, because she models it for me so consistently.

Ode to Jessica *by Angie Pedersen*

This punchart was inspired by Mary Englebreit. To make the half-circle, I traced a large cottage cheese container lid and cut out the large circle. I chalked the middles and edges of the flowers for definition.

SUPPLIES: Paper is by Northern Spy. Lettering template is by ProvoCraft. Font is Arial by Monotype and CK Cursive by Creating Keepsakes.

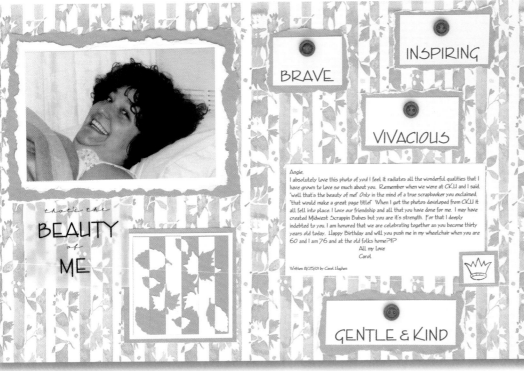

BRAVE

INSPIRING

VIVACIOUS

that's the BEAUTY of ME

Angie,
I absolutely love this photo of you! I feel it radiates all the wonderful qualities that I have grown to love so much about you. Remember when we were at CKU and I said, 'well that's the beauty of me' Only in the mind of a true scrapbooker you exclaimed, 'that would make a great page title!' When I got the photos developed from CKU it all fell into place. I love our friendship and all that you have done for me. I may have created Midwest Scrappin Babes but you are it's strength. For that I deeply indebted to you. I am honored that we are celebrating together as you become thirty years old today. Happy Birthday and will you push me in my wheelchair when you are 60 and I am 76 and at the old folks home?!?
All my love
Carol
Written 8/25/01 by Carol Hughes

GENTLE & KIND

The Beauty of Me *by Carol Hughes*

Carol created these pages as a birthday gift for me. It lists several words that Carol associates with me and also includes a letter she wrote. Carol mimicked the background paper pattern with her punchart accent.

SUPPLIES: Paper is by Susan Branch. Punches are Birch (mini and medium) and Maple Leaf (small and medium) by Family Treasures. Font is Enviro.

WWW.

Friendship quotes at the International Friendship Day site:
www.friendship.com.au/quotes/

Friendship quotes:
www.geocities.com/Heartland/Farm/9753/poem_files/friends2.htm

Quotes on kindness and giving:
www.inspirationpeak.com/kindness.html

Some neat friendship images here—print them out and include them on a layout:
www.wickedmoon.com/friendship.html
wickedmoon.net/cards/friendship/advicemountains.jpg
wickedmoon.net/cards/friendship/girlsbridge.jpg
wickedmoon.net/cards/friendship/dirt.jpg
wickedmoon.net/cards/friendship/friendshipwithoneself.jpg
wickedmoon.net/cards/friendship/angelfriends.jpg

8: TEAM PLAYER

Definition of this role:

This section looks at what kinds of groups you join, what you do with those groups, the level of your participation, and how being a member of a group has affected your life.

Being a part of a group offers a sense of belonging, a feeling of welcoming acceptance. Participating in a group often engenders lasting friendships. Groups offer a forum for individual involvement and leadership, often with great personal rewards.

Ask yourself, "What does it mean to be a member of a team? What reward does group membership offer me?" You could also look at why particular groups are so dear to you. What is it about those groups that allows for, and even encourages, a level of intimacy and belonging that other groups don't? What piece of yourself does belonging to a group speak to?

Within the activities of a group, you define yourself as a team member. You might think and act differently within the dynamics of a group. Perhaps participating in a group brings out strong leadership or organizational qualities in yourself that don't surface when you're alone. This role is also important because the groups you join say a lot about your personal interests and priorities. Joining a group is a conscious decision. Your choices dictate how you spend your free time, and give voice to what matters deeply to you.

In my scrapbook...

I journaled about the variety of different groups I have joined in my life, from high school to present day, giving dates of my participation. I talked about what I did as a part of each group, who I met and spent time with, what leadership positions I held, my duties as a part of those positions, and what techniques and skills I learned while I participated in each group. I included group photos, photos of individual friends I made and photos of group activities.

In 1999, I met several ladies on a scrapbooking mailing list on the Internet who all lived in Arkansas. I was so excited to discover that several of them lived in Northwest Arkansas. Little did I know at the time that some of these ladies would become my best friends. We started getting together on a monthly basis to crop, but it turned into so much more than that. We started another email list so that we can keep up with each other's lives, and we call ourselves the "NWAGang." We all have small children, and many of us are stay-at-home moms. Aside from our monthly crops, we have playgroups, parties, and "field trips." Our children and husbands all get along as well. When Logan died, these girls were there for me like no one else. They gave us money, brought us dinner, and were just there to listen when I needed to cry. I really couldn't ask for a better group of friends.

The Gang *by Libby Weifenbach*

Are you part of a scrapbooking group? Libby chose great colors and used a multitude of squares to celebrate her group. In her journaling, Libby talks about when she was introduced to the group, how they quickly became friends, their similar interests and how they helped her through a hard time. This layout really communicates how important being a member of "The Gang" is to Libby.

SUPPLIES: Vellum is by DMD Industries. Lettering template is PC Blocky by ProvoCraft. Punches are Square by Emagination, Circle by Family Treasures and Alphabet punches by EK Success. Font is LD Diary by Lettering Designs.

Prompts to trigger journaling

- What groups have you joined? Give dates of participation for each group. Consider groups based on:
  - o Your church
  - o The Internet
  - o Local hobby groups
  - o Local advocacy groups
  - o Physical fitness
  - o Schools
  - o Neighborhoods
  - o Parenting
  - o Support groups
- Why do you join groups? What rewards do you receive?

- How do you volunteer to help the group? What leadership positions have you held? What are or were your job duties?
- What friends have you made through groups?
- What group do you wish you had joined or could have joined? Why didn't you?
- Where have you traveled with the groups you have joined?
- How often does the group meet? What do you do at meetings?
- What have you learned as a result of participating in a group? Skills? Techniques? Life lessons?

Never doubt that a small group of thoughtful committed people can change the world: indeed it's the only thing that ever has!

—Margaret Meade

A little group of wise hearts is better than a wilderness of fools.

—John Ruskin

Something special happens when people laugh together over something genuinely funny, and not hurtful to anyone. It's like a magic rain that showers down feelings of comfort, safety and belonging to a group.

—Mary Jane Belfie

Metro Scrappers *by Melissa Abbe*

Without realizing it, Melissa used the Acrostic writing exercise (similar to the one featured at www.inspire2write.com) to help her create the title. What a fun and enlightening way to describe her group. What words can you think of to describe a group you're in? Melissa also journaled about when she joined, how important the group has become to her and some of the group's activities.

SUPPLIES: Paper is by Paper Patch. Circle punch is by Family Treasures; corner punch is by Emagination. Hair is made with Tracerkins by EK Success. Title font is CK Chunky Block by Creating Keepsakes (printed backwards and cut out); journaling fonts are CK Primary and CK Print by Creating Keepsakes.

Service to others is the rent you pay for your room here on earth.

—Muhammad Ali

I shall pass through this world but once. Any good therefore that I can do or any kindness that I can show to any human being, let me do it now. Let me not defer or neglect it, for I shall not pass this way again...

—Mahatma Gandhi

Photo opportunities

❏ Group photos for each association.

❏ Photo of you at a group activity.

❏ Photo of a meeting.

❏ Photo or scan of the group mascot or logo.

❏ Photo of you with close friends from the group.

Ideas for memorabilia

❏ A meeting agenda.

❏ A group activity calendar.

❏ Ticket stubs from outings.

❏ Samples from group demonstrations.

❏ Minutes from a meeting.

❏ E-mails from group members.

I Didn't Find My Friends, God Gave Them to Me
by Carol Hughes

Carol started an online e-mail list for scrapbookers in the Midwest. This layout describes the group's growth and how much the group means to her. She included a group photo to depict the significant number of happy scrapbookers in the heartland.

SUPPLIES: Vellum is by Susan Branch and Paper Garden. Punches are Poinsetta by Family Treasures and Flower Pot by Emagination. Chalk is by Craf-T Products. Title font is Girls are Weird from onescrappysite.com; journaling font is CK Journaling by Creating Keepsakes.

CADENCE SONGS 2000-2001
- CHATTANOOGA CHOO CHOO
- BRUSHSTROKES • LINDEN LEA
- THE GIFT TO BE SIMPLE
- APPLE TREE WASSAIL • BLESSING
- I'M A WOMAN • PSALM 150
- SET ME AS A SEAL • THE BELLS
- COME CELEBRATE THIS DAY
- NURSERY RHYMES • ALL THAT JAZZ
- CHARIOT CHILDREN • JINGLE BELLS
- I DON'T WANNA WALK WITHOUT YOU
- SHOO SHOO BABY • A LA RU
- STORMY WEATHER • MR. SANTA
- HARK THE HERALD ANGELS SING
- TOMORROW SHALL BE MY DANCING
- O LITTLE TOWN OF BETHLEHEM DAY
- ALL ALONE BENEATH THE MISTLETOE
- BUSHES AND BRIARS
- THE STAR SPANGLED BANNER

MY FAVORITES:
SHOO SHOO BABY
ALL THAT JAZZ

CADENCE PERFORMANCES/ EVENTS
SEPT. 21 - RETREAT
OCT. 13 - FACE PAINTING @ RIVER-
OCT. 25 - 1ST SCHOOL CONCERTFEST
NOV. 6 - ICE CREAM BASH
DEC. 7 - STAR SPANGLED BANNER
     AT BASKETBALL GAME
DEC. 13 - WINTER CONCERT
DEC. 18 - BOYS IN MEN'S CHOIR
     JOIN US TO SING AT ROSE
     CREEK ELEMENTARY
DEC. 21 - BLUFFDALE ELEMENTARY
OTHER XMAS PERFORMANCES FOR
WARDS, ETC
FEB. 6 - SCHOOL SOLO + ENSEMBLE
FEB 16 + 17 - RENAISSANCE FEAST
FEB 27 - JOINT CONCERT @ WOODS
MAR. 7 - REGION SOLO + ENSEMBLE?
MAR. 28 - MARCH MADNESS CONCERT
APR. 6-9 - TOUR!

CADENCE MEMORIES

PERFORMANCES/EVENTS CONT.
APRIL 25 - REGION FESTIVAL
MAY 12 - STATE FESTIVAL
MAY 14 - CHOIR BANQUET
MAY 16 - FINAL CONCERT
MAY 17 - CADENCE OPERAH

MY FAVORITE MEMORIES
OF BEING IN CADENCE
• THE ALTOS ALWAYS DOING
  BETTER THAN THE SOPRANOS
• WHEN WILLY WOULD TELL
  US TO MIX UP INO DIFF.
  PARTS, AND ME AND
  CHRISSY WOULD JUST
  SWITCH SPOTS.
• ME AND CHRISSY DOIN'
  LINDY WHEN WE WERE
  BORED.
• HAVING "GIRL TALK" WITH
  CAROLINE AND AUBREY
• ME AND MORGAN
  LAUGHING AT WILLY:
  "WHAT WAS THAT??" SIT
  DOWN!
• SINGING 'LET IT SNOW
  AND DOING A STRIPTEASE
  WITH CHRISSY, HEIDI, +
  CANDICE AT THE ICE CREAM
  BASH
• PASSING NOTES BACK AND
  FORTH WITH WILLY AT THE
  WOMEN'S CHORAL FESTIVAL
• AND MY FAV? THE
  MUSIC WE MADE TOGETHER

Cadence Memories *by Erica Shaw*

While Erica could have written a long paragraph, the bullet journaling is much more effective. By using bullets, Erica singles out each song, performance and miscellaneous thoughts to make each component of this memory significant. Most likely, 10 years from now many of these memories would be forgotten. All of this information also shows how busy this group keeps Erica (can you believe that she's still just a teenager?)

SUPPLIES: Patterned paper by Fiskars. Pens by Stampin' Up!. Colored pencils by Colorific.

The path is long,
Let us walk together.
The times are difficult,
Let us help each other.
The way is joyful,
Let us share it.
As life opens before us,
Let us begin.
—Unknown

Alone we can do so little; together we can do so much.
—Helen Keller

In American society today, we need to have volunteerism. I truly believe that it is the glue that will hold us together and it will be the energy that will take us to the 21st century.
—Barbara Mikulski

Every problem that the country faces is being solved in some community by some group or some individual. The question is how to get connected so that the whole nation can solve problems.
—George Bush, Sr.

The best memories are often made of good friends, good food, and a little slice of time to be together.
—Hallmark card

I am proud to be a member of a party that opens its doors to all men—and closes its hearts to none.
—Lyndon B Johnson

A community is like a ship; everyone ought to be prepared to take the helm.
—Henrik Ibsen

WWW.

Search YahooGroups for an e-mail list on scrapbooking. Try searching for your city and/or state at:
groups.yahoo.com/
search?query=scrapbooking

Resources for meeting other moms in your area:
www.onescrappysite.com/
momresc.htm

Find scrapbooking clubs at ScrapLink.com:
www.scraplink.com/
clubs.htm

Moving to a new city? Check out this site to meet new people in your area:
www.newcomersclub.com/
index.html

Flexible volunteer opportunities available across the country:
www.citycares.org/national/

Gather your local scrapbooking group to support the Picture Me Foundation:
www.pictureme.org/
support.htm

Amy Kreeger, Michelle Johnson, and Diane Saftic model the rolled-brim caps they knit for a co-worker expecting triplets!

Jessica Eastin shows a strawberry cap and a sock, both projects in progress.

Diane Saftic shows off a Debbie Bliss pattern pillow that she's knitting for her living room.

Knit On! *by Jessica Eastin*

When these four ladies found out they all enjoyed knitting, they decided to form an impromptu knitting circle. They meet every other week to work on their individual projects. Jessica's journaling talks about how much she enjoys these evenings and the fact that they aren't the stereotypical group of knitting grannies. They are all highly educated scientists!

SUPPLIES: Paper by Mary Engelbreit. Hand knitted swatch. Kabob sticks for needles. Font is CK Journaling by Creating Keepsakes.

Amy Kreeger knit these striped socks.

Okay, Brett Phillips isn't actually a knitter and he's not in our knitting group, but Elizabeth posed him for this photo when they discovered the fruit caps that Jessica has knit by the dozens as baby gifts for sale for $20 apiece. (One of my friends said she saw similar caps in a high-end baby boutique for $40 each! Ouch!)

One of my favorite groups is my knitting circle. There are four of us, all passionate about knitting. We meet about every other week, less regularly in the summer, alternating houses for dinner and an evening of knitting together. Sometimes we all road trip out to Lawrence, Kansas to our favorite yarn store, the Yarn Barn. I don't think we fit the stereotypical group of knitting grannies. All four of us are in our late 20's/mid 30's and professionals in science-related fields. Between the four of us, we all have either master's level degrees or professional school degrees. There is a chemist, a pharmacist, a geologist, and an environmental scientist, all happily knitting together.

9. WORKER BEE

Through the daily tasks, projects, and long-term goals defined in the workplace, you establish another portion of your identity. When the work is stimulating, and the environment is empowering, a job can be a fulfilling part of your life.

If you don't enjoy your work, your scrapbook layouts can help you define what kind of work you would prefer or even just vent about what you don't like about your job. You can create your dream job by piecing it together on a scrapbook page.

You also have the opportunity to pick out the parts of your current job you do appreciate, and highlight them as an accentuation of the abundance in your life. Whatever your employment situation, this section of The Book of Me can illustrate what you find most satisfying about working.

The jobs you choose say a lot about who you are and how you would like to be perceived. For the most part, you choose your job(s) because of your talents and interests—you bring your own unique spin into any workplace.

Your self-confidence stems in part from your perception of how well you do your job and how much of a challenge it presents you.

In my scrapbook...

I talk about my time spent teaching preschool and how that affected my current parenting theories and techniques. I included journaling about how I had to switch gears and work as an administrative assistant when teaching did not pay well enough.

I journaled about how it felt to give up teaching and retrain my focus toward organizing other people's lives and workplaces. I included photos of

Definition of this role:
This section provides a place for you to describe the various jobs you have held over the years, why you chose a particular job, and what you liked most about it.

Teacher *by Toni Patton*
This layout is one adapted from a page design shown by Lisa Bearnson on QVC. Toni made the apples by tracing on the backside of cardstock with a punched apple and then tearing them.

SUPPLIES: Title font is LD Fill-In; journaling font is Cricket.

The secret of joy in work is contained in one word—excellence. To know how to do something well is to enjoy it.
—Pearl Buck

I never feel age...If you have creative work, you don't have age or time.
—Louise Nevelson

The sweat of hard work is not to be displayed. It is much more graceful to appear favored by the gods.
—Maxine Hong Kingston

Real success is finding your lifework in the work that you love.
—David McCullough

Decide what you want, decide what you are willing to exchange for it. Establish your priorities and go to work.
—H. L. Hunt

It is impossible to enjoy idling thoroughly unless one has plenty of work to do.
—Jerome K. Jerome

Don't say you don't have enough time. You have exactly the same number of hours per day that were given to Helen Keller, Pasteur, Michelangelo, Mother Teresa, Leonardo da Vinci, Thomas Jefferson, and Albert Einstein.
—Louise Nevelson

different work assignments and of me working at the computer.

Prompts to trigger journaling

❑ Describe different jobs you've had. Explain the work duties, when you worked there, your wages, the length of your commute, the work attire.

❑ What did you like best about each job?

❑ Who did you meet at each job? Did you see each other outside of work?

❑ If you could have five other lives or careers, what would they be? Describe your duties in a day. What would your salary be?

❑ How would you run a company differently from your employers?

❑ What have you been able to accomplish in your job(s)? What do you wish you were able to accomplish?

❑ What have you learned at each different job site? Describe the skills and techniques.

❑ What is your idea of "success" in your job? How close are you? What would it mean for you to be "living the good life"? How does your job contribute to that? Is it the actual work or is it just the paycheck?

Yes, that's a bottle of wine. It's a birthday gift for AFTER work.

Cake is a big behind-the-scenes part of pharmacy.

I received my bachelor's degree in Biology from the University of Missouri in Columbia in 1986 and went on to study pharmacy at the University of Missouri-Kansas City. I met Mike while doing a pharmacy internship at the VA Hospital, so I guess you can say that pharmacy brought us together! After receiving my pharmacy degree in 1989 and becoming dually licensed in both Kansas and Missouri, I went to work full time in a retail setting for Osco Drugs. After finally becoming a mom in late 1995, I decided to try part-time work in order to stay home and enjoy motherhood fully. This has been the best career decision for me. I love being a pharmacist and I especially love that I can work part time. Pharmacy has been such a perfect profession in that respect. I only work two days a week, about 20 hours a week, so I consider myself a stay-at-home mom, but after five days of doing "mom stuff," I put on my lab coat and go off to do pharmacy stuff. I enjoy the balance of home life and my professional career. I really feel blessed to have the best of all possible worlds.

Rx: Pharmacist *by Jessica Eastin*

Jessica commemorates her 12-year career as a pharmacist with this sharp layout. Her journaling talks about how pharmacy has been the best career for her and how blessed she feels to be able to be both a part-time pharmacist and a stay-at-home mom. The pictures of her workplace give insight into how much fun she has at work and how much she enjoys her job.

Supplies: Stickers are by Frances Meyer. Lettering is by Accu-Cut. Font is CK Journaling by Creating Keepsakes.

Photo opportunities

❑ Photo of your work building from the outside.

❑ Photo of your desk, office or workspace.

❑ Photo of you doing your job or different tasks throughout the day —take pictures of a "day-in-the-life" of your job.

❑ Photos of your co-workers.

❑ Photos of all the different machines you use in your job: computer, fax machine, copier, scanner, postage meter, phone, etc.

Ideas for memorabilia

❑ Pocket page for your resume, business card or company brochure.

❑ Copy of a day's appointments from your planner.

❑ Color copy or scan of your company ID tag or badge.

❑ A paystub or timeslip.

❑ Printout from the company website (including logos).

❑ Recipes for food you've taken to work functions or recipes shared by co-workers.

Do not wait; the time will never be "just right." Start where you stand, and work with whatever tools you may have at your command, and better tools will be found as you go along.

— Napoleon Hill

Begin where you are; work where you are; the hour which you are now wasting, dreaming of some far off success may be crowded with grand possibilities.

—Orison Swett Marden

Be glad of life because it gives you a chance to love and to work and to play and to look up at stars.

—Henry Vandyke

My Version of Hell *by Kellie Reardon*

While this layout doesn't go into what Kellie hated about his job, it's obvious she was relieved to be done. The items she points out illustrate that she needed many things to comfort her throughout the work day. The photos of her workspaces also give a glimpse of the workplaces of our times, making an interesting historical commentary.

Supplies: Embossed paper is by K&Co. Cardstock is by Bazzill Basics. Stickers are by David Walker for Colorbok. Eyelets are by Impress. Pen is by Sakura. Colored pencils are by Lyra Rembrandt.

WWW.

JobWise articles and resources at MomsOnline:
momsonline.oxygen.com/
jobwise/

Discussion board for working women trying to organize their homes:
pub2.ezboard.com/
ftheunofficialsheboard
shesonthepayroll

Mothers At Home offers strategies for transitioning to at-home parenting:
www.mah.org/media/
Media_pr_trans.htm

Balancing work and family at iVillage:
www.ivillage.com/topics/
work/work/
0,10707,166534,00.html

Staying connected with your kids while working:
www.networkingmoms.com/
StayingConnected.html

Managing multiple priorities by Dr. Don Wetmore at One Scrappy Site:
www.onescrappysite.com/
homeorg/wetmore-
time.htm

Search for work-related clipart at Microsoft's clipart gallery (search for "work", "paperwork" or "offices"):
dgl.microsoft.com/

Santa on Call *by Jessica Eastin*

Jessica's mother was called upon to fill in for a sick Santa and hand out treats to children in the hospital. This story gives a glimpse of Joan's dedication and good nature, characteristics that serve her well as a hospital social worker.

SUPPLIES: Paper is by Keeping Memories Alive. Letter stickers are by Creative Memories. Lettering is by ABC Tracers. Punch is by Paper Shapers. Font is CK Journaling by Creating Keepsakes.

Sparkles *by Angie Pedersen*

This layout is further proof that if you don't have photos of a specific time in your life, you can make up for it in other ways. I didn't take any pictures when I was working in this store, so I went back and took pictures specifically for this layout. For a little more interest, I created a shaker box of "sparkly things." I could also have included by store ID tag, a time slip or a paycheck stub.

SUPPLIES: Letter stickers are from Debbie Mumm by Creative Imaginations. Pen is from Zig. Shaker box idea originated from Rhonda Solomon.

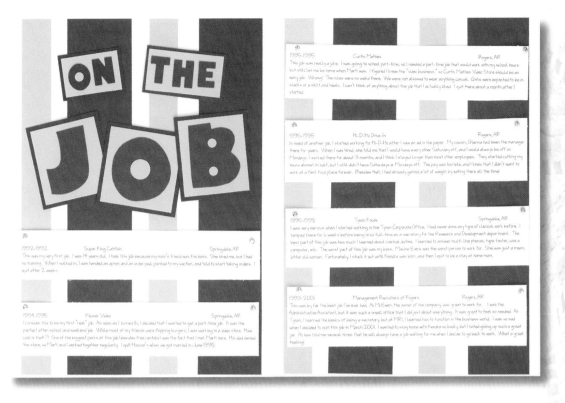

On the Job
by Libby Weifenbach

Here is another layout with no photos that is still a very strong page design. Note the use of cardstock to create a striped background. Libby's journaling lists the dates of each job, where she worked and the city. Then she gives a bit of insight into what kind of work she did and what she liked and disliked about each job.

SUPPLIES: Lettering template is Spunky by DJ Views. Circle punch is by Family Treasures; Alphabet punch is by EK Success. Font is CK Penman by Creating Keepsakes.

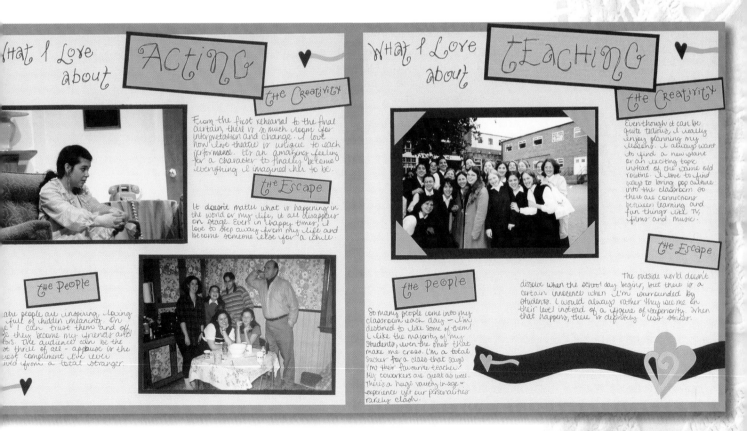

What I Love About... *by Shimelle Laine*

These layouts could easily be stand-alone, one-page layouts but are so interesting together because Shimelle uses the same subheadings for each job she holds. Both teaching and acting offer her a creative outlet, the opportunity for escape and access to inspiring interesting people. Note that Shimelle used her own handwriting.

SUPPLIES: Punches by PaperShapers and EK Success. Pens by Zig and EK Success.

10: CHARACTER

Definition of this role:

From this chapter on, we move to an introspective approach. The role of Character is based on your individual priorities and core values—your personal philosophy that directs your behavior and attitude. This section is based on Stephen Covey's *7 Habits of Highly Effective People.*

Words to Live By
by Angie Pedersen

Reading Stephen Covey's *7 Habits of Highly Effective People* was significant in my personal growth. This page tells about how the book affected me. The green flowery paper represents growth and the *Words to Live By* from Susan Branch illustrated many principles described by Covey. This layout uses the same hidden journaling technique as used in the "Ally" example on page 36. The page protector is adhered to the card using Pioneer Memory Mounting Taper double-sided tape.

SUPPLIES: Paper is by Susan Branch for Colorbok. Font is Joplin by Bright Ideas.

Stephen Covey, author of *7 Habits of Highly Effective People,* teaches you to "identify the first, most important roles, relationships, and things in your life—who you want to be, what you want to do, to whom and what you want to give your life, the principles you want to anchor your life to, the legacy you want to leave."

Covey suggests brainstorming "what matters most" in your life and offers a differentiation. "*Values* are the things that are important to us. *Principles,* on the other hand, are guidelines for human conduct." Through the lessons offered in the *7 Habits* book, you can pinpoint your core values, defining for yourself where you want to focus your energies and where your priorities lie.

In creating scrapbook pages honoring these values, you reinforce who you are. You realize that you are a model to your children and an inspiration to your friends. It makes your priorities concrete.

Designing a layout, gathering supplies and photos, and journaling will reinforce your convictions and reiterate the lessons you want to pass on to others. And by using photographs of yourself and your personal journaling, you will see yourself as a strong individual, a person that you may not realize you were. You will see proof that you are a person of character.

Once you recognize yourself as a person of character and define what matters most in your life, you are in a better place to share this wealth with those around you. You will create meaningful pages that will be treasured by your family because they embody your very essence. They will be pages created from your heart. Think about all the time and love you pour into your pages about other people's activities. Now consider giving just a portion of that attention to yourself.

In my scrapbook...

I really enjoyed the process of identifying my values and wrapped myself in the depth of the project. I dug deep for the reasons why these things were so important to me and what about them struck such a deep chord.

I included the insights gained from reading *7 Habits* in my own scrapbook. I titled the section, "Angie as a Woman of Character." Each page in the section highlights the cornerstones in my personal philosophy and describes how I bring them to life, including real-life applications. I did pages on "Encouragement," "Courage," "Personal Growth" and "Love." These four tenets make up what I value most and I use them to guide my decisions and actions.

Once I defined my core philosophy in life, I was able to imagine what my life could ideally be like. Covey suggests creating "clarifying statements," defining how you can live out a principle and stating it in positive, present tense terms.

I visualized myself living within each core principle. What would I do if I lived according to the principle of encouragement? What would I like to accomplish for myself within that principle? Then I stated this image in positive, present tense terms: "I actively seek out opportunities to encourage others to meet their plans, goals and dreams, and hearten them through dark times." Another "clarifying statement", for the principle of Courage, reads: "I face my life with all its rewards and challenges, to the best of my abilities."

You too can be a person of character! You too have gifts to offer your friends and family. You too may be a source of inspiration to others. You too have a story to tell.

Personal Growth
I strive to achieve my potential in the social, emotional, mental and spiritual realms. I seek out situations when I can facilitate this process in others.

This photo was taken in October 1988 at a youth group spiritual retreat at Camp Chippewa. I always felt such spiritual renewal after these retreats, and really infused with the Spirit.

Personal Growth
by Angie Pedersen

I wanted to highlight the value I place on personal growth and how important continual development is to me. I used a photo taken at a spiritual retreat to illustrate my desire to grow spiritually as well as mentally and emotionally.

SUPPLIES: Background paper is by Colors By Design; Plaid mat is by Keeping Memories Alive. Title font is CK Flair by Creating Keepsakes; journaling font is Joplin by Bright Ideas.

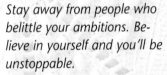

I am a firm believer that all of us to a very large extent are truly masters of our own health, happiness, success, and destiny in life simply by the thoughts we think... the words we speak... and the actions that we take.

—Tom Bennett

When you are content to be simply yourself and don't compare or compete, everybody will respect you.

—Lao Tzu

Winning doesn't make you a better person, but being a better person makes you a winner.

—Unknown

With each choice you make, you create your life.

—Unknown

Stay away from people who belittle your ambitions. Believe in yourself and you'll be unstoppable.

—Emily Guay

Do not attempt to do a thing unless you are sure of yourself; but do not relinquish it because someone else is not sure of you.

—Stewart White

Life is not easy for any of us. But what of that? We must have perseverance and, above all, confidence in ourselves. We must believe that we are gifted for something, and that this thing, at whatever cost, must be obtained.

—Marie Curie

There comes a time when you have to stand up and shout:
This is me damn it! I look the way I look, think the way I think, feel the way I feel, love the way I love! I am a whole complex package. Take me... or leave me. Accept me—or walk away! Do not try to make me feel like less of a person, just because I don't fit your idea of who I should be and don't try to change me to fit your mold. If I need to change, I alone will make that decision.

When you are strong enough to love yourself 100%, good and bad—you will be amazed at the opportunities that life presents you.

—Stacey Charter

In the midst of winter, I finally learned that there was in me an invincible summer.

—Albert Camus

Too many people overvalue what they are not and undervalue what they are.

—Malcom Forbes

We are what we repeatedly do. Excellence, then, is not an act, but a habit.

—Aristotle

I care not what others think of what I do, but I care very much about what I think of what I do! That is character!

—Theodore Roosevelt

Prompts to trigger journaling

❑ What are the key lessons you want to pass on to others? How can you best depict the lessons you want to teach your children?

❑ What do you believe in? What do you stand for? Think of a noun that describes those priorities.

❑ Pin down what it is about certain activities that you value.

❑ Do you volunteer because you believe it is important to give back to the community? Perhaps service or generosity is a core part of your belief system.

❑ Do you value excellence or growth?

❑ Define your priorities by what gives you a sense of peace, joy and security in your life.

❑ Consider a person you admire. What is it that you admire? What qualities do you wish to incorporate into your own life?

❑ What principles speak to you? Why and how are these your priorities?

❑ What anecdotes from your life illustrate what's most important to you?

❑ Possible core values:
  o Creativity
  o Development of talents
  o Empowerment
  o Encouragement
  o Excellence
  o Fairness
  o Faith
  o Friends or friendship
  o Growth
  o Honesty and integrity
  o Love
  o Patience
  o Perseverance
  o Service
  o Trustworthiness

Encouragement
by Angie Pedersen

One of my core principles is Encouragement. My "clarifying statement" says it all: "I seek out opportunities to support others in their plans, goals and dreams and to hearten them through the rough spots in their lives."

I used a fairy godmother paper-piecing to illustrate my desire to help others make their dreams come true. I used a picture of me at a staff meeting for scrapbook instructors at a local store because, as an instructor, I strive to encourage people to believe in their own creativity.

Supplies: Paper is by Susan Branch for Colorbok. Punches are Jumbo Circle by Family Treasures and Primitive Star PaperShaper for EK Success. Paper-piecing pattern is by Jennifer Balckham, downloaded from www.scrappershaven.com. Title font is CK Flair by Creating Keepsakes; journaling font is Joplin by Bright Ideas.

Photo opportunities

❑ Photo of you with your children, family, or the people to whom you are leaving your life lessons.

❑ Photo of site of volunteer or charity work.

❑ Photo of your church ("service", "stewardship," "faith").

❑ Photo of you studying or of your school ("excellence," "growth").

❑ Photo of your mother or grandmother (mentor for "patience" or "love").

❑ Photo of you laughing ("joy," "laughter" or "sense of humor").

❑ Photo of you teaching a child to tie his shoe ("patience"—also include a shoelace!).

❑ For my Encouragement page, I included a photo of me with two other instructors from a local scrapbooking store. In my classes, I encourage people to try new techniques and cultivate their own creativity.

❑ Photo of you scrapbooking ("creativity", "family").

Ideas for memorabilia

❑ Encouraging e-mails you've sent or received.

❑ Heartfelt notes you've written and received.

❑ Something that symbolizes the love you've given in your life.

❑ For my page on the principle of Courage, I included an essay I wrote on a particularly trying time in my life—I included over 12 pages of typed text in a pocket page (see below).

❑ Brochures for charity to which you contribute.

❑ College transcript or grade card ("excellence," "growth," "development of talents").

Treat people as if they were what they ought to be, and you help them to become what they are capable of being.

—Goethe

What do we live for it if is not to make life less difficult for each other?

—George Eliot

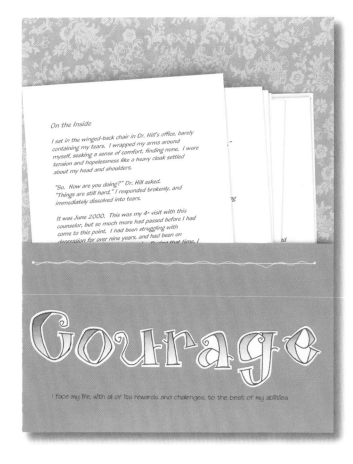

On the Inside

I sat in the winged-back chair in Dr. Hill's office, barely containing my tears. I wrapped my arms around myself, seeking a sense of comfort, finding none. I wore tension and hopelessness like a heavy cloak settled about my head and shoulders.

"So. How are you doing?" Dr. Hill asked.
"Things are still hard," I responded brokenly, and immediately dissolved into tears.

It was June 2000. This was my 4ᵗʰ visit with this counselor, but so much more had passed before I had come to this point. I had been struggling with depression for over nine years, and had been on...

Courage *by Angie Pedersen*

The essay in the pocket describes a time when my courage was tested and how I rose to the occasion. The layout represents to me the idea that I can face true hardship and survive intact. I chose the stormy blue colors to reflect life's hardships.

SUPPLIES: Paper is by Mini-Graphics. Title font is CK Flair by Creating Keepsakes; subtitle font is Joplin by Bright Ideas; journaling font is Blacklight downloaded from www.onescrappysite.com.

Courage

I face my life, with all of its rewards and challenges, to the best of my abilities

WWW.

Let Franklin Covey take you step-by-step through the value-defining process: www.franklincovey.com/ missionbuilder/

User notes from reading *7 Habits*: userpage.fu-berlin.de/ ~tanguay/7habits.htm

ABC list of Highly Effective Educators: www.itrc.ucf.edu/ conferences/abc.html

Bill Ferguson's ground rules for living: www.effectiveliving.com/ groundrules.htm

Search Bartlett's Quotations: www.bartleby.com/100/

Quotations home page, searchable by subject: www.geocities.com/~spanoudi/ quote.html

Little Miss Liberty paper doll pattern, used on Encouragement layout: www.scrappershaven.com/ creativersity/missliberty.htm

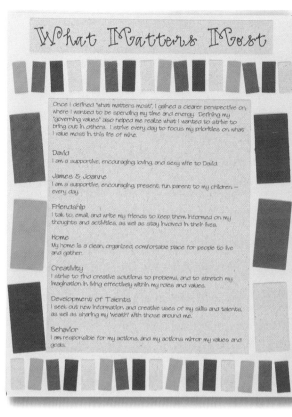

What Matters Most
by Angie Pedersen

This layout comes from an exercise I did while reading *7 Habits of Highly Effective People.* Covey suggests to identify the key parts of one's life and then imagine the epitome of successful living as related to each key part. I pinpointed the things that were most important to me by thinking about my days and what I generally wished I was doing. I thought about who I wished I was spending my time with and how I most wanted to spend my time. Then, I thought about what I would ideally do in each situation. Now it's here for me, whenever my goals or priorities become hazy or misplaced.

Supplies: : Rectangle punch is by Family Treasures. Title font is DJ Sweet by DJ Inkers; journaling font is Joplin by Bright Ideas.

And the Greatest of These Is... Love
by Angie Pedersen

Love is a guiding force in my life. I try to temper my decisions and actions with love and consider loving options for my treatment of others. I'm not saying it happens all of the time, but even recognizing that a loving attitude is important to me colors my perspective and influences my behavior. This photo reflects the love I feel for my family and the joy I feel when I am with them.

Supplies: Paper is by ProvoCraft. Title font is Bradley Hand by ITC; "Love" type is Lucinda Handwriting by Bigelow & Holmes; journaling font is Joplin by Bright Ideas.

11: A WORK IN PROGRESS

Up until now, we've focused on your unique blessings and gifts and on your strengths and talents. But all of us are also "works in progress."

Several friends have asked me what I mean by this phrase. My friend Libby wondered if that meant future goals to accomplish, or if the phrase means how one has grown by way of past experiences.

A work in progress encompasses the idea of self-growth. It could cover past, current or goals for future personal growth. The main goal is to see your stories preserved.

My friend Sarah told me that she always considers herself a work in progress and that she hesitated working on this section because preparing a layout felt so final, like she was done progressing. Your pages don't have to be a final say. You can use those pages as a time line to show your progress along the road of self-improvement. Just keep updating your progress as you change your goals and as you move forward.

In my scrapbook...

I talked about my struggles with depression and how that has made me a stronger person. I also based a page on a quote from Oprah Winfrey's magazine on the idea of re-inventing oneself, and then journaled about how I am in the continual process of reinventing myself and how I go about that process.

Definition of this role:

This section looks at how you view change and crisis in your life, and how it has changed you. You'll define the parts of your life that need reinventing, and how you might go about the process. Use this section as a catalyst for change—plan your self-improvement and set your goals.

THE JOURNEY

I SUPPOSE I'VE ALWAYS HAD "ISSUES" WITH MY WEIGHT. I WASN'T NECESSARILY OVERWEIGHT AS A CHILD, BUT I WASN'T EXACTLY PETITE EITHER. BY THE TIME I REACHED JUNIOR HIGH SCHOOL, I WAS IN SIZE 8-10 JEANS. I FELT HUGE! I SOON BECAME SOMEWHAT OBSESSED WITH LOSING WEIGHT. TO THIS DAY, I'M NOT SURE WHAT MADE ME DO IT. I BELIEVE I WAS BORDERLINE ANOREXIC. I PRACTICALLY STOPPED EATING, AND WHEN I DID EAT, I FELT HORRIBLY GUILTY. I DIDN'T TAKE ME LONG TO LOSE A LOT OF WEIGHT. MY SIZE 3 JEANS WERE TOO BIG FOR ME. MY MOM WAS TERRIFIED. I LATER FOUND OUT THAT MY FRIENDS HAD ACTUALLY CALLED MY MOM AT WORK BECAUSE THEY WERE CONCERNED ABOUT ME. THE WORST PART WAS THAT, EVEN AT 100 POUNDS, I FELT SO FAT. I COULDN'T UNDERSTAND WHY MY MOM WAS ACTING LIKE SHE WAS. IN MY MIND, I WAS DOING NOTHING WRONG. I DIDN'T UNDERSTAND THE DANGER THAT I WAS PUTTING MYSELF IN

I STAYED AT A WEIGHT OF APPROXIMATELY 105 POUNDS UNTIL I MARRIED MARTI IN 1995. THEY SAY THAT MARRIAGE ALWAYS PUTS ON THE POUNDS, AND THAT WAS DEFINITELY TRUE IN MY CASE. I WAS SO HAPPY BEING MARRIED TO MARTI THAT I TOTALLY FORGOT ABOUT FEELING FAT. THAT, ALONG WITH MY JOB AT A FAST FOOD RESTAURANT, PUT MY WEIGHT AT ABOUT 125 POUNDS WITHIN 6 MONTHS.

BY THE TIME I GOT PREGNANT WITH KENDRA 2 YEARS LATER, I WAS UP TO 142 POUNDS. I KNEW I WAS OVERWEIGHT, BUT I JUSTIFIED IT BY TELLING MYSELF THAT I WAS TRYING TO GET PREGNANT. I FIGURED I'D LOSE THE WEIGHT AS SOON AS I HAD A BABY. LIKE A LOT OF WOMEN, I GAINED ADDITIONAL WEIGH WITH PREGNANCY. I WEIGHED 170 WHEN I DELIVERED, AND MOST OF THAT WEIGHT STUCK WITH ME FOR A FEW YEARS AFTER KENDRA WAS BORN.

IN THE SUMMER OF 2001, I DECIDED THAT SOMETHING HAD TO BE DONE ABOUT MY WEIGHT. I WEIGHED 165, AND I WAS MISERABLE. I HATED LOOKING IN THE MIRROR (SEE PICTURE TO THE LEFT TAKEN JULY 2001). I KNEW I HAD TO FIND A PROGRAM TO HELP ME. I REMEMBERED MY STRUGGLE AS A TEENAGER, AND I DIDN'T WANT TO FALL INTO THAT TRAP AGAIN. A FRIEND TOLD ME ABOUT WEIGHT WATCHERS, SO I WENT TO THE WEBSITE TO GET SOME INFORMATION. I WAS THRILLED TO DISCOVER THAT THEY HAD AN ONLINE PROGRAM! THAT MEANT I WOULDN'T HAVE TO GO TO MEETINGS!! I SIGNED UP THAT DAY, AND I HAVEN'T LOOKED BACK. I LOVE THE POINTS PROGRAM BECAUSE I CAN STILL EAT ALL OF MY FAVORITE FOODS WITHOUT THE GUILT. MY MOM IS DOING IT WITH ME, AND I THINK THAT MAKES IT EASIER. AT 12 WEEKS, I'VE LOST ABOUT 20 LBS, AND I COULDN'T BE HAPPIER. I'M LEAVING A SPACE AT THE TOP OF THIS PAGE FOR A PICTURE OF ME AT MY GOAL WEIGHT. I HOPE TO BE ADDING THAT SOON!

Space reserved for "After Picture"

GOAL WEIGHT: 125

DATE ACHIEVED: _____

COMMENTS: _____
_____
_____

The Journey
by Libby Weifenbach

This was obviously not an easy layout for Libby to do. Weight is such as personal subject. But it was important for her to process these feelings and thoughts to pin down the best and healthiest course of action. Note the space Libby left for her "after" photo. What an inspiring and motivating gesture!

Supplies: Title font is LD Fill-In; journaling font is Cricket.

Finish each day and be done with it. You have done what you could. Some blunders and absurdities no doubt crept in; forget them as soon as you can. Tomorrow is a new day; begin it well and serenely and with too high a spirit to be cumbered with your old nonsense.

—Ralph Waldo Emerson

The only difference between success and failure, is the ability to take action!

—Alexander Graham Bell

Life is 50% change and 50% coping. You have to learn to bend and remember to smile.

—Unknown

In the pursuit to better ourselves we are sure to encounter failure. Going on after each failure is how character is built.

—Allan L. Barr

Change is constant, progress is optional.

—Unknown

Wherever you find a successful person, you will find a person who has struggled in his or her life. Life is a struggle and the rewards go to those who meet difficulty face to face, overcome it, and move on to the next challenge.

—Daniel Tan

Prompts to trigger journaling

❑ What have you learned from crises in your life? What have you overcome?

❑ When in your life have you experienced the most growth?

❑ What's the hardest thing you've ever done?

❑ What have you missed out on simply because you were too afraid of what others would think if you stepped away from them?

❑ Complete this statement: "I need to change..."

❑ What perceptions do you have of yourself that only you know?

❑ How would you like to reinvent yourself?

❑ What would you like to let "die" in your life? And what would you like to fill the void?

❑ What do you need to clear from your path?

❑ Complete this statement: "When I think about really getting my life in order, I..."

❑ "When one door of happiness closes, another opens; but often we look so long at the closed door that we do not see the one which has been opened for us." (Helen Keller) What closed door do you keep staring at?

❑ Complete this statement: "Change brings..."

❑ Complete this statement: "I am..."

❑ Complete this statement: "I am meant to be..."

❑ Complete this statement: "I would like to give more time and effort to..."

❑ If you were to die in a year and were able to make amends to all you needed to, who would you make amends to?

❑ What is your worst habit?

❑ Complete this statement: "To find my own balance, I..."

❑ Include friends' thoughts on your self-improvement efforts.

❑ What do you actually have control over?

❑ List five best pieces of self-improvement advice you've received from friends or mentors.

Stop Juggling & Start Living
by Linda Kempf

Linda is working with Cheryl Richardson's book, *Life Makeovers*. She's scrapbooking the whole process—each exercise that Richardson suggests, the major themes for each chapter and how she is putting these ideas to work in her life. Most people could come up with a list of balls they are juggling as well as a list of balls they'd like to drop. How is your sense of balance in your life a work in progress?

SUPPLIES: Paper is by Doodlebug Design. Circle Punches are by Marvy. Font is Snap by ITC.

Photo opportunities

❑ Photo of you at a self-improvement seminar or class.

❑ Photo of you taken at the same age as a time of personal growth.

❑ Photo of a person who models personal growth or self-improvement for you.

❑ Photo of a self-help guru whose books you love.

Ideas for memorabilia

❑ Ticket stubs to enlightening lectures you've attended.

❑ Color copies or scans of covers of your favorite self-help or self-improvement books.

❑ Helpful articles or essays you've torn out of magazines, pieces that have led to an "a-ha moment" for you. Consider color copying several of them to use as background paper.

The important thing is not to stop questioning.
— Albert Einstein

The way to get good ideas is to get lots of ideas and throw the bad ones away.
—Linus Pauling

All my limitations are self-imposed and my liberation can only come from true self-love.
—Max C. Robinson

A strong woman isn't afraid of anything ... but a woman of strength shows courage in the midst of her fear.
— Unknown

Because my children insist on growing up, my parenting skills and techniques are constantly a Work in Progress. James & Joanne daily provide me with parenting (and personal) challenges, and I must rise to meet that challenge. In college I majored in early childhood education, so I thought I would be well-trained for parenthood. In many situations I was. I knew what was typical development for different ages, and how a child processes through things cognitively. But parenting these two active children has really forced me to think outside my textbooks! I have to continually work at keeping myself informed of current ideas on child development. I seek out other moms for ideas and support, and talk to my mom and mother-in-law to see what has worked for them. The better parent I become, the more I can give my children.

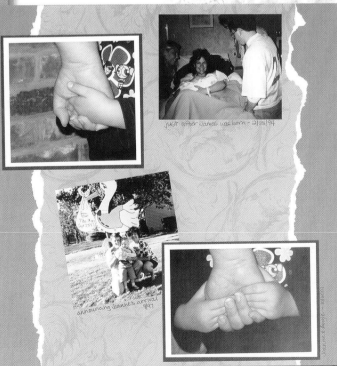

Growing Up Together *by Angie Pedersen*

I figured that this could be one of the last occasions that I can tell my children to come hold my hand for a picture and not get a look like, "You're crazy if you think I'm going to do that!" (Even though I was pushing it for my 7-year-old!) I love this layout for the photos and the simplicity—the page went together quickly because it's just torn paper and straight matting. The whole page makes me smile.

SUPPLIES: Paper is by Anna Griffen. Lettering template is Fat Caps by Frances Meyer. Flathead studs are by Bedazzler. "Growing Up" font is Gigi by Esselte Corp.; journaling font is ZiptyDo by Adobe.

WWW.

Personal growth and self improvement:
www.selfgrowth.com/

"Reinvention" article:
www.oprah.com/
omagazine/200101/
omag_landing_200101.html

Read Life Coach Cheryl Richardson's ideas on improving your life:
www.cherylrichardson.com/
newsletters/newsletter-
week2.html

Staying positive when feeling incompetent:
www.yourpotential.com/
article/positive_1.html

Rosie O'Donnell on depression:
www.rosiemagazine.com/
causes/9_rosie.html

Marie Osmond on postpartum depression:
www.abilitymagazine.com/
osmond.html

How others have overcome adversity:
www.chickensoup.com

Exercises for personal development:
www.centerforpersonal
reinvention.com/
excercise_1.htm

Using a journal in times of personal crisis:
www.writersdigest.com/
journaling/articles/
0401shelter.html

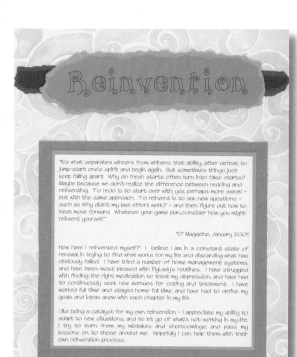

Reinvention *by Angie Pedersen*

I found this neat quote in the January 2001 issue of *O Magazine*. The quote fit perfectly with my frame of mind at the time. It summed up the kind of growth I was seeking and the kind of quantum-level changes I was trying to make. The quote became the basis for the page, then I wrote about why it was so powerful to me and how I was putting those kinds of ideas into play in my life.

Supplies: Paper is Blue Swirl by Sonburn. Title font is CK Celebration by Creating Keepsakes; journaling font is Joplin by Bright Ideas.

Bad Habits *by Sarah Plinsky*

Sarah made a list of her three worst habits (to her). She wrote out the pros and cons for each of them and printed the bad habits on vellum. She attached the vellum printouts as pockets, using eyelets at the corners. Then she stuck some of the pros and cons in the respective pockets. Her journaling box describes her reflection on this exercise. Note how her sense of humor plays into her self-improvement process.

Supplies: Paper is by Karen Foster. Vellum is by Close to My Heart. Cardstock is by Bazzill Basics. Eyelets are by Impress Rubber Stamps. Title font is CK Block by Creating Keepsakes; journaling font is Wednesday by Journaling Genie Software.

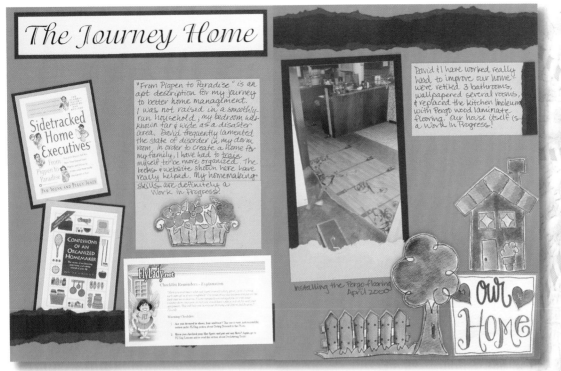

The Journey Home

"From Pigpen to Paradise" is an apt description for my journey to better home management. I was not raised in a smoothly-run household; my bedroom was known far & wide as a disaster area. David frequently lamented the state of disorder in my dorm room. In order to create a home for my family, I have had to train myself to be more organized. The books & website shown here have really helped. My homemaking skills are definitely a Work in Progress!

David & I have worked really hard to improve our home. We've retiled 3 bathrooms, wallpapered several rooms, & replaced the kitchen linoleum with Pergo wood laminate flooring. Our house itself is a Work in Progress!

Installing the Pergo flooring
April 2000

The Journey Home
by Angie Pedersen

Do you have books that have helped you reach a goal? I scanned the covers of influential home management books and printed them out. Then I did a screen capture of a home management website by pressing the "Prt Scrn" key on my computer keyboard when I was at the screen I wanted to print. This copied the image on my screen to the clipboard. Then, I opened MS-Publisher and pasted the image onto the workspace.

SUPPLIES: Diecuts are "Our Home" Fresh Cuts by BumperCrops. Font is Adorable by MicroLogic Software.

"If you want to be somebody else,
If you're tired of fighting battles with yourself,
If you want to be somebody else,
Change your mind."
Song by Sister Hazel

Most people who know me, even in passing, think of me as optimistic, competent, outgoing and enthusiastic. Understandable, as that's largely how I present myself. That's what I want people to think of me. But what most people don't know, however, is how hard it is for me to be that person, sometimes.

Since 1990, I have struggled with how I perceive my accomplishments and myself. The roar of my critical inner voice can sometimes be deafening. I often view myself through a sort of distorted haze. I dismiss my accomplishments as commonplace; I believe I should have done more or better, and then feel guilty for my "failures." Then I assume other people make similar judgments.

But because I am strong, I am trying to fight those automatic thoughts. My attitude is something I can control. I can choose to call a halt to the "stinkin' thinkin'" that pops into my head. I can work to consciously replace it with more encouraging phrases that offer me more hope than despair. Because I continually strive to maintain a rational and positive mindset, my mental health is a Work in Progress. I read a lot about cognitive therapies, which help me reframe my automatic critical thoughts with more "rational" thought processes. (You can see on this page the covers of some books that have really helped me). I go to a group discussion on such practices every Tuesday night. And I seek professional help when I can't do it on my own.

The phrase "It's all in your head" often has a negative connotation, meaning that whatever you're feeling is just your imagination, that it's not real. I prefer another meaning. I have the power to create a healthy, positive attitude. It's "all in my head."

All in My Head *by Angie Pedersen*

To create the "photo booth" style photos, my husband took a series of pictures of me with a digital camera. I just stood there and made faces—what fun! Then, I uploaded the photos to my computer and edited them with PaintShop Pro. I filled the images with a shade of brown for a "sepia" look and then printed them onto photo paper. I scanned the book covers and printed them also on photo paper.

SUPPLIES: Cardstock paper by Bazzill Basics. Brads by American Tie & Fastener. "All in My" title font is Bergell LET by Esselte Letraset; "Head" title is Vino Bianco by ITC; journaling font is Joplin by Bright Ideas.

12: PERSONAL POWER

Definition of this role:

In this section, you will learn how to use affirmations for personal growth. To affirm something is "to state it as truth." Affirmations are powerful because they are framed in the present-tense. You envision the end result before any of the work has been done.

Decide what kind of person you want to be, what kind of characteristics you want to personify, what kind of goals you want to achieve—then imagine yourself as that person. Describe that person in positive present-tense phrases.

Professional life coach Cheryl Richardson calls this setting an "internal goal; one that focuses on how you'll develop yourself personally or strengthen your character." She also refers to this process as "strengthening yourself from the inside out."

Psychotherapist Rosemary Mazurek suggests writing a positive statement about yourself at the top of a page. You may write, "I am a strong person who is capable of many fine deeds." Beneath this statement, list five to ten things that happen in a day.

Consider scrapbooking this exercise. Select a quality you want to develop and show yourself becoming that person. Think about the good, solid decisions you have already made in your life, decisions such as leaving a stressful job or marriage, or deciding which college to attend. What hard choices have you already made that turned out well? Did you choose to sever a toxic relationship or relocate for an opportunity?

Find photos of yourself during the time you made a difficult decision and create a page detailing your options, how you thought your way through it, whose advice you sought and any other resources you drew upon during your decision-making.

The finished pages will be a tribute to your own growth and wisdom.

I Am Brave by Angie Pedersen

Well, I didn't have any pictures of me "being strong" and I couldn't think of any to go take. So I thought of someone who represented strength to me—Wonder Woman. Talk about a strong female character. I found these images on the Internet and printed them out onto photo paper. I used the vellum and gold cord to represent her golden lasso and power bracelets.

SUPPLIES: Gold wired cord by Offray. Title font is Easter Parade by Harold Lohner; journaling font is Joplin by Bright Ideas.

I Am Beautiful
by Angie Pedersen

My husband and kids frequently tell me I'm pretty or beautiful but I have a hard time believing it when it's just me and the mirror. So, I found a picture of me from a time when I felt like I looked good and I was happy (I was with my kids and headed out on a date with my husband). Then I gave the page a simple design to keep the focus on the photo.

SUPPLIES: Paper is by ProvoCraft. Title font is CK Celebration by Creating Keepsakes; journaling font is Joplin by Bright Ideas.

If you can imagine it, you can achieve it. If you can dream it, you can become it.
—William Arthur Ward

People become really quite remarkable when they start thinking that they can do things. When they believe in themselves they have the first secret of success.
—Norman Vincent Peale

We are what we think about all day long.
—Ralph Waldo Emerson

I figured that if I said it enough, I would convince the world that I really was the greatest.
—Muhammad Ali

You can be greater than anything that can happen to you.
—Norman Vincent Peale

Act as if you were courageous. This makes you a bit braver as if one side of yourself had been challenged and wished to show it was not wholly afraid.
—Dale Carnegie

Life isn't about finding yourself. Life is about creating yourself.
—George Bernard Shaw

The best way to predict your future is to create it.
—Unknown

I Deserve Gold Stars!
by Angie Pedersen

When my close friend Carol Hughes first said this phrase to me, I knew I had to make a layout of it. It takes me back to my childhood days when a teacher would give me a gold star for being good or trying hard. Fast forward about 15 years and I was the one giving out the gold stars to my students. I love the idea of offering someone praise and recognition for effort and hard work.

SUPPLIES: Paper is by Keeping Memories Alive. Gold wire is by Artistic Wire. Gold acrylic star jewels are by The Beadery. "I Deserve" title font is DTC Brody M31 by Digital Type Corp.; "Gold Stars" title font is Twinkle by Bright Ideas; journaling font is Donny's Hand from PrintArtist by Sierra Online.

If you want to develop courage, do the thing you fear to do and keep on doing it until you get a record of successful experiences behind you. That is the quickest and surest way ever yet discovered to conquer fear.
—Dale Carnegie

We would accomplish many more things if we did not think of them as impossible.
—Chretien de Malesherbes

In my scrapbook...

I included affirmations such as "I am beautiful," "I am strong," and "I am brave." It was not easy creating pages for these positive images because I didn't fully believe them yet. But I found some good pictures and did the best I could. I also found images who model ideals, like Wonder Woman for my "I Am Brave" layout.

Prompts to trigger journaling

❑ Consider what success means to you. What will your life look like when you are successful? What clothes will you wear? What will your philosophies on life be? How will you speak?

❑ In Chapter 2 of *Life Makeovers*, Cheryl Richardson asks: What quality would you like to develop more of...? How do you need to grow? What shortcomings would you like to improve upon?

❑ What ideal behaviors, attitudes and values do you admire in other people? Why do you want those things for yourself? How can you tell, for example, when someone is confident? What advice do you think your mentors might offer?

❑ How far are you from your ideal self? Look at the differences between your "now" self, and your ideals. Consider the steps you

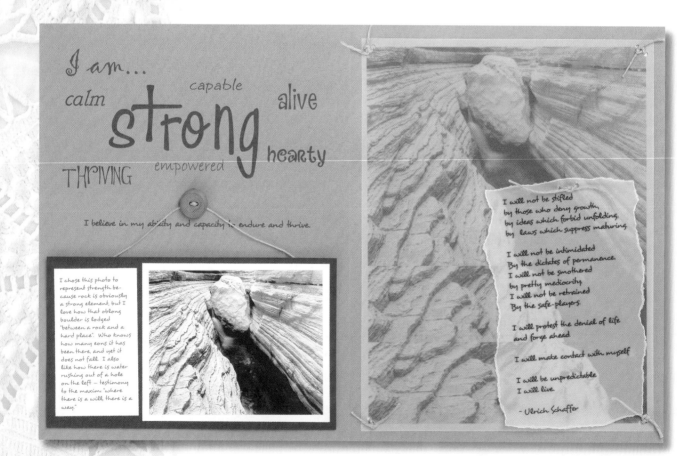

I Am Strong by *Angie Pedersen*

Again, I had trouble finding a photo of me being "strong," so I searched the Internet for an image that represented strength to me. I found this black and white photo at a professional photographer's site (www.harrington.com). I chose this one because not only is it a beautiful photo,

rock is a strong element. I also love how the boulder is lodged "between a rock and a hard place." This is a testimony to the strength and enduring beauty of nature.

SUPPLIES: Photo copyright 1998 Roy Harrington; www.harrington.com. Button is by Create-a-Craft. Journaling font is Desyrel by Dana Rice & Apostrophic Labs.

could take to close the gap. What would you have to do to effect those changes?

❑ How are you already living the life of your ideal self? Think of examples from your daily life when you are confident, beautiful, content or financially responsible, for example.

❑ What are the obstacles to your becoming this ideal person or possessing your ideal qualities? What has inhibited you in the past? How can you overcome them now? Make a mental change in how you see obstacles or challenges—they are opportunities for growth! Think positively.

❑ How would your life be different if you did possess these ideal qualities? How would you act differently? How would you think differently? How would you treat other people? How would other people treat you? What would your children think? How would it affect your relationships?

Affirmation examples

In her book *Unlocking the Power Within*, journaling instructor Shifra Stein suggests this exercise to get started in the practice of writing affirmations for yourself:

❑ Write down five positive affirmations that begin with "I can."

❑ Write down five positive affirmations that begin with "I am."

❑ Write down five positive affirmations that begin with "I know."

❑ Write down five positive affirmations that begin with "I deserve."

To use this exercise in scrapbooking, write your affirmations, then find or make your own examples of putting these words into action. When you scrapbook pages on positive qualities you have developed, you are proving to yourself that you've done it once and you can do it again.

WWW.

Tap into the power of your mind—writing positive affirmations:
www.womanlinks.com/
health/
health092301.shtml

Daily positive thoughts delivered right to your e-mailbox:
free-positive-thought.com/

I Can! Online article about using positive thinking:
www.icanonline.net/
channels/
self_discovery/self-
awareness/
grow_stronger.cfm

Article on developing positive self-esteem:
www.positive-way.com/
self-esteem%20what%
20is%20it.htm

The role model oath:
www.self-worth.com/
rolemodel.htm

The ABCs of positive thinking:
www.self-worth.com/
foodfor5.htm

Gratitude *by Angie Pedersen*

I sometimes have trouble seeing past the crisis of the moment to the genuine blessings already present in my life. To bring a sense of security and serenity to my perspective, I created the affirmation, "I already have everything I need to be genuinely happy." I used entries from my Gratitude Journal to prove the validity of the statement and scrapped it with some of the prettiest paper I have.

SUPPLIES: Paper is by Anna Griffin. Chalk is by Craf-T Products. Pop-dots are by All-Night media and Therm-O-Web. Title font is CK Celebration by Creating Keepsakes; subtitle font is DJ Sweet by DJ Inkers; journaling font is Donny's Hand from PrintArtist by Sierra Online; "entries from" font is Bradley Hand by ITC.

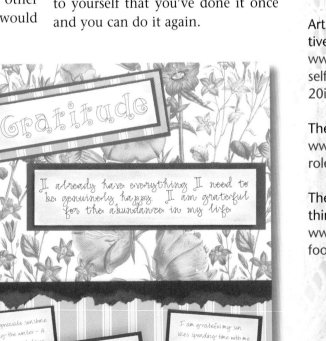

13: DREAMER

Definition of this role:

This role allows you to envision and plan for all the hopes and goals you have for your own future. This role also allows you to develop your creative, abstract imagination when you consider "what-if" kinds of situations.

The movie, "Field of Dreams," offered the advice, "If you build it, they will come." This section follows that advice by providing a place for you to record all the dreams you would like to bring to fruition.

If you build the foundation for your dreams, your dreams will come true. It's amazing how much you can accomplish when you make a list for yourself. I made my list of "25 Things to Do in My Lifetime" in April, 2001, and achieved three of them by September, 2001!

Here are two ways of handling the "task list of a lifetime:"

1. Write or print out a list of 25 dreams or goals. Then, create a layout for each dream once the dreams are accomplished. Put them behind your original "to-do" list.

2. Create a layout per dream ahead of time, leaving room for photos and journaling once the dream is accomplished. This format might be best presented as a separate scrapbook for this theme.

You can also imagine what your life would be like if... all sorts of things! What if you go back to school? What if you learn another language? What if you take gourmet cooking classes? What if you move to a different part of the country or world?

Have fun with these kinds of imaginative exercises. They might just show you a fertile imagination you never realized you had. You might also realize how blessed your life is right now,

Dreams... *by Shimelle Laine*

The journaling on the white vellum documents the basic things that Shimelle wants to achieve. The "bitten" bits on burgundy vellum have dream quotations and sayings that inspire her. Shimelle knows them well enough that she doesn't need to see them fully to think them in her head.

SUPPLIES: Cardstock is by Paper Accents. Burgundy vellum is by Pixie Press; white vellum is by Worldwin. Pens are by Zig, EK Success, Ultimate Glitter Gel Pens and American Crafts. Photo is by Fred Murphy.

all because of decisions you did make in the past. Gather all your ideas in a brainstorming session, then scrap a page about all of your ideas!

We all have dreams for our lives, things that we hope someday to see happen. But for some people, dreams remain only that. Dreams become goals when you have a plan. Once you take the time to plan, and lay the foundation for your dreams, you are one step closer to making them a reality.

In my scrapbook...

I printed out a list of 25 Things to Do in My Lifetime, and included a photo of one of the places I want to visit. Another layout features a picture of me pointing to an article in *Creating Keepsakes* scrapbook magazine that mentions my website. Another layout highlights a trip I took with my husband to Paris (a dream realized and a dream to go again in the future).

Prompts to trigger journaling

❑ Make a list of 25 Things to Do in My Lifetime. These can be practical and attainable, or fanciful and unrealistic. Consider including dreams that you have already accomplished—that's one you can cross off your list right now!

❑ What trips have you dreamed of taking? Who would you take with you? What sites would you see?

Writing down your dreams and aspirations is like hanging up a sign that says, 'Open for Business.'
—Henriette Anne Klauser

Dreams are the touchstones of our character.
—Henry David Thoreau

Whatever you can do, or dream you can, begin it.
—Goethe

Reach high, for stars lie hidden in your soul. Dream deep, for every Dream precedes the goal.
—Vaull Starr

DREAMS
Do Come True

To my Dad

You inspired the Dream. You were my inspiration. As a child, I watched you go to college at night. I remember you in your recliner with a card table on your lap, studying. I remember stacks of computer punch cards – and when you completed the course, you let your girls play with them. I remember your graduation and my first "store bought" dress. Thanks for being my inspiration.

To my Children

May we three, Grandpa Bob, Terry and I serve as an inspiration. May you follow your Dreams, pursuing them and letting nothing get in your way. I wish for you happiness – in your life, in your job, in the things that you do. Do them to the best of your ability. Take pride in working hard. Be honest and forthright. Have integrity. Dream big dreams but don't neglect the little ones. Speak the Truth. Care for others; have compassion. Follow your heart. Walk with the Lord daily.

Know that I LOVE YOU!

To my Husband

You nurtured the Dream. You were truly the wind beneath my wings. You supported me, encouraged me and provided me the opportunity to finish. I remember your struggle to complete your degree - I am so very proud of you for being the first in our family to accomplish the goal. Thanks for your love and support.

Follow your

DREAMS
Wherever They Lead

Dreams *by Cathy Gray*

At her graduation party, Cathy toasted her loved ones featured in this layout. No pictures were taken during the toast (Cathy is usually the one to take pictures), so she used pictures from her graduation day to document the toast.

SUPPLIES: Punch is Star by All Night Media. Font is CK Columns, Script and Print, by Creating Keepsakes.

Dreams are... illustrations from the book your soul is writing about you.
　　　　　　—Marsha Norman

Twenty years from now you will be more disappointed by the things that you didn't do than by the ones you did do. So throw off the bow-lines. Sail away from the safe harbor. Catch the trade winds in your sails. Explore... Dream... Discover.
　　　　　　—Mark Twain

Only as high as I reach can I grow,
Only as far as I seek can I go,
Only as deep as I look can I see,
Only as much as I dream can I be.
　　　　　　—Karen Ravn

To dream of a different tomorrow,
to search for a brighter star...
achieving life's heights and horizons
begins from where you are!
　　　　　　—Unknown

You Have So Much
You have powers you never dreamed of.
You can do things you never thought you could do.
There are no limitations in what you can do
except the limitations in your own mind
as to what you cannot do.
Don't think you cannot.
Think you can.
　　　　　　—Darwin P. Kingsley

❑ Who have you dreamed of meeting? Why do you want to meet this person? How has he or she influenced your life? What would you ask him or her?

❑ What crafts or techniques have you always wanted to try? What skill do you dream of learning? Knitting? Piano playing? Soapmaking? Sewing? Eating with chopsticks?

❑ Do you have any physical goals, like losing a significant amount of weight or training for a marathon? Why are these goals important to you?

❑ If you could travel back in time, what time period would you choose? Why? Who would you like to meet? What would you wear? Where would you live? What kind of work would you do?

❑ Make a list of all the reasons you've been unable to achieve your dreams in the past. Now come up with ways to overcome them.

❑ Rich Little created the word "sniglet" to define words that are not commonly found in dictionaries, but the world "needs" anyway. What "sniglet" do you have the need to create?

❑ If you won the lottery, what would you do with the money? How much would you save and how much would you spend? What would you spend it on, or whom? What financial worries would winning the lottery alleviate?

A Dream Realized: Broadway
by Sarah Plinsky

One of the things on Sarah's "to-do" list was to see a show on Broadway. When this dream came true, she created this layout to celebrate. Sarah included the playbill from the show, used the font "Broadway" and recreated the Broadway lights with a yellow vellum circle-punched border.

Supplies: Vellum is Parchlucent by Paper Adventures. Punch is by Family Treasures. Font is Broadway by URW Software.

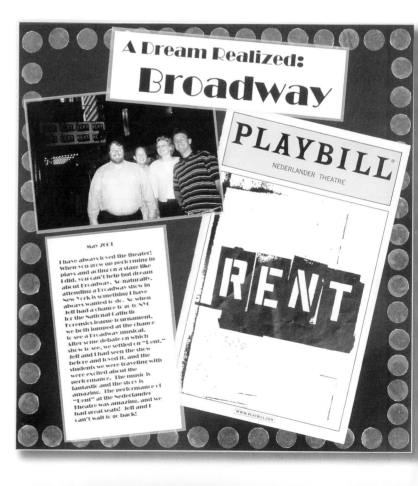

Photo opportunities

❑ A photo of you at graduation.

❑ Photos of you training for, and then after running a marathon, or climbing a mountain or finishing a bike race.

❑ Photos of you before and after some accomplishment (weight loss, getting in shape, etc.).

❑ A photo of you meeting an idol or mentor.

❑ A photo of you taking a class in something you've always wanted to learn, or the finished product after learning the new skill.

❑ A photo of you taken on location of a dream travel destination.

Ideas for memorabilia

❑ Color copies or scans from travel brochures for trips you dream of taking.

❑ Scans from travel books or website printouts for sites you'd like to see.

❑ Printout of your 25 Things to Do in My Lifetime list.

❑ Ticket stubs to a show or a concert you've always wanted to see.

❑ Lottery ticket.

❑ Autograph from an idol or mentor.

❑ Recipe for a dish you ate while traveling on a dream vacation.

Life is an opportunity, benefit from it.
Life is a dream, realize it.
Life is a challenge, meet it.
Life is a promise, fulfill it.
— Unknown

Within your heart keep one still, secret spot
Where dreams may go
And, sheltered so,
May thrive and grow.
— Driscoll

Don't be afraid of the space between your dreams and reality. If you can dream it, you can make it so.
— Belva Davis

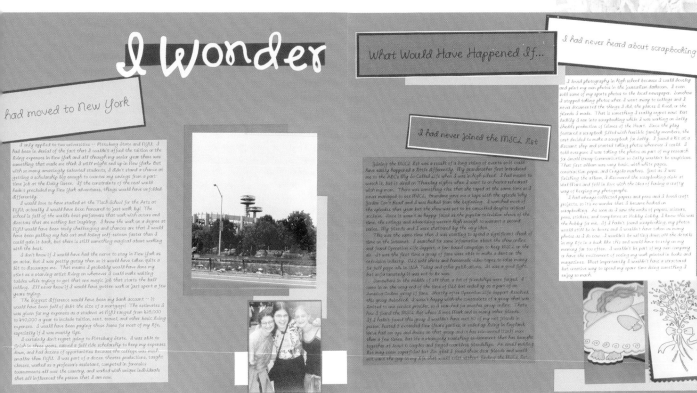

I Wonder What Would Have Happened... *by Shimelle Laine*

In her extensive journaling, Shimelle proposes how her life would have been different is she had made different choices or if certain opportunities had not been available to her. This "what if" perspective is interesting for seeing the turning points in her life. It also helps her realize how many blessings are in her life now as a result of her decisions.

Supplies: Font is CK Pretty by Creating Keepsakes.

www.

Write down your goals to make them more real (and attainable):
www.about-goal-setting.com
/Step2.htm

Goal-setting articles by professional coaches:
www.ihavegoals.com/
public/articles/
article_focus.asp

Ten most important things to do today to help achieve your goals:
successnet.org/articles/
angier-TTmostimportant.htm

Top ten things to "ask" of your goals:
www.philiphumbert.com/
Articles/
10AskYourGoals.html

This article answers the question: Why is it important to have a dream?:
www.dreamsalive.com/
wisdom5.htm

Read about travel destinations around the world:
www.ricksteves.com/

Learn how to do all sorts of interesting things:
www.soyouwanna.com/site/
info/azlisting.html
www.learnto.com/browse/
all_2torials.asp

Spa Nut *by Jessica Eastin*

One of Jessica's dreams is to "go to a spa for a few days and be pampered non-stop with decadent spa treatments." Until she gets to go on this dream trip, this layout shows how she pampers herself at home.

SUPPLIES: : Background paper is by Autumn leaves; vellum is by Paper Pizazz. Oval, circle and flower punches are by Family Treasures; "pom" PaperShaper is by EK Success. Diecut letters are by Accu-Cut. Chalk is by Craf-T Products. Bathtub and towel paper-piecing pattern is by Gillian Greding, www.two peasinabucket.com. Font is CK Journaling by Creating Keepsakes.

25 Things to Do in My Lifetime *by Angie Pedersen*

I made this list over the course of a week, just jotting down ideas of things I would like to do or accomplish at some point in my life. One of my dreams is to take my kids to DisneyWorld, so I included a photo taken on my honeymoon at Cinderella's Castle. I could also have pulled an image off of a website to illustrate other goals. For example, for "to be a guest on Oprah," I could print off her logo or signature from her website.

SUPPLIES: Title font is DJ Sweet by DJ Inkers; journaling font is Joplin by Bright Ideas.

14: SPIRITUAL BEING

Spirituality contributes to your sense of identity, your sense of security, even your sense of purpose in life. Spirituality, for many, answers a great deal of questions and provides comfort in dark times.

Some people practice the religious teachings of their childhood. Others seek out what best fits them as adults. Everyone has a spiritual component to their lives, whether practiced in a group setting or not.

Use this section to map out your "spiritual heritage." This heritage includes your religious experiences from childhood, your questionings of young adulthood, and what you are practicing or experiencing now.

Describe how you came to your current beliefs and values and how they affect your day-to-day choices and decisions. How important is your faith to you? How does it play itself out in your interactions with your family, your friends and with strangers? How has your faith influenced the person you are today?

The journaling prompts are non-denominational and address various aspects of spiritual life, such as service or charity, religious philosophy, and spiritual mentors who have shaped your perspective.

In my scrapbook...

I created a two-page spread on the role youth group played in my high school years. I journaled about the friends I made, the leadership roles I filled and the summer camp I attended. I included photos of me with youth group friends, and a photo of me taken at the same age I attended summer camp. I also did a layout about a time of questioning in my life, when I turned to a good friend and spiritual advisor for counsel.

Definition of this role:
This section looks at how you feel a spiritual influence in your life and what you do because of it.

One in Spirit
by Angie Pedersen

This layout honors a woman whose spiritual guidance influenced my faith journey. I was glad to have saved the letter she wrote me—her words are still comforting to me. Note the variety of techniques including the mixture of fonts, crumpled cardstock used as a photo mat and a page protector pocket page adhered with Bedazzler studs.

SUPPLIES: Diamond cut studs by Bedazzler. Title font is LOT Pioneer by Leaves of Time; journaling font is Joplin by Bright Ideas.

Faith is the daring of the soul to go farther than it can see.

—William Newton Clark

Arriving at the fundamental truth that God is everywhere is the purpose of spiritual life, and each stage of God takes us on a journey whose end point is total clarity, as sense of peace that nothing can disturb.

—Deepak Chopra

The various religions are like different roads converging on the same point. What difference does it make if we follow different routes, provided we arrive at the same destination.

—Mahatma Gandhi

Truth rises from the silence of being to the quiet, tremendous presence of the Word. Then, sinking again into silence, the truth of words bears us down into the silence of God. Or rather God rises out of the sea like a treasure in the waves, and when language recedes his brightness remains on the shores of our own being.

—Thomas Merton

One cannot help but be in awe when he contemplates the mysteries of eternity, of life, of the marvelous structure of reality. It is enough if one tries merely to comprehend a little of this mystery every day. Never lose a holy curiosity.

—Albert Einstein

Prompts to trigger journaling

❑ What was your religious education as a child?

❑ Who were the mentors and teachers who shaped your beliefs about the world, God or Divinity, and your relationship to it? When did you meet them? Where? What lessons did they teach you? Did they teach in a formal classroom setting or by life example?

❑ As a child, what did you consider to be the nature of God, (i.e. the visual images you associated with God)? How has that changed?

❑ Has your path changed since childhood? Think about times when your beliefs changed and what prompted those changes. For example, you may have changed churches because there were more people your own age in the new church or you may have embraced a new faith.

❑ Do you currently participate in a religious group? How long have you been a member? What do you like most about the congregation? What kind of activities do you participate in?

❑ Do you have friends or relatives that practice a different faith than you? Do you ever have theological discussions? What do you admire about their beliefs and faith practices?

Joyful Noise *by Libby Weifenbach*

Libby commemorates the role gospel music has played in her spiritual life. Her journaling talks about when she realized how important music is to her and her family and how honored she was to record a gospel album with her mother. Note the crisp lines of this layout and how striking the red, black and white look together.

SUPPLIES: Stickers are by Frances Meyer. Lettering is by Accu-Cut. Font is CK Journaling by Creating Keepsakes.

- ❑ What scriptures do you find inspiring or uplifting? What beliefs or readings help you during dark times?

- ❑ Define what "spiritual experience" means to you. Write about a spiritual experience you have had outside of a religious setting.

- ❑ How has your faith sustained you through hard times?

- ❑ What beliefs, values and principles guide your actions and decisions?

- ❑ What experiences have you had that you attribute to a higher power?

- ❑ What role does forgiveness play in your faith? Who do you need to forgive?

- ❑ Talk about your belief or disbelief in spirits or angels. Have angels played a role in your life? How?

- ❑ Describe unconditional love. Describe an experience you have had with unconditional love.

- ❑ What are you thankful for? Describe the role gratitude plays in your life. Do you keep a gratitude journal? What do you include in it?

- ❑ What do you think about capital punishment?

Be kind, for everyone you meet is fighting a battle.
—John Watson

Faith is to believe what you do not yet see; the reward for this faith is to see what you believe.
—St. Augustine

The best portion of a good man's life is the little, nameless, unremembered acts of kindness and love.
—William Wordsworth

Good Works *by Angie Pedersen*

The journaling in this layout talks about the role mission trips played in my spiritual journey. I had only one photo of us embarking on a mission trip, so I filled the rest of the space with photos of my church and one of the church's stained glass windows. The title was created by typing the text into the WordArt tool in MS-Publisher, reversing it, and printing it out onto the backside of the patterned paper.

SUPPLIES: Flip-over Frame-Ups frame by My Mind's Eye. Title font is Bohemian Garden Party by Blue Vinyl fonts; journaling font is Tempus Sans by ITC.

WWW.

Craft a "spiritual time line:"
www.angelfire.com/journal/
inspirare/junetime.html

Sacred texts from over 10
different religions:
www.beliefnet.com/help/
link_directory.asp

World prayers:
www.worldprayers.org/
index.html

Guideposts:
www.guideposts.org/

Thought-provoking ques-
tions (and answers):
www.zukav.com/frames/
qa_index.htm

Online fellowship, friendship and inspiration:
ChristianMom
www.christianmom.com/
index.html

Define your spiritual
priorities with this quiz:
www.spiritualityhealth.com/
newsh/bigtest/bigtest.cgi

Jewish Scrappers online:
www.geocities.com/
jewishscrappersresource/
groups.yahoo.com/group/
jewishscrappers

Christian Scrappers online:
groups.yahoo.com/group/
ChristianScrappers
groups.yahoo.com/group/
Christian-scrappers
www.chartingthejourney.com
I%20Remember%
20When/remember.htm

❑ If you could ask God five questions, what would they be? Or
what conversation would you like
to have with God?

❑ What do you pray about? Do you
have any favorite prayers?

Photo opportunities

❑ Photo of the religious building of
your childhood.

❑ Photo of the religious building
you attend now.

❑ Photo of your religious leader.

❑ Photo of any extracurricular religious groups you attend, like
a women's circle, bible study or
prayer group, sports teams, book
discussion group.

❑ Photo of church activities, like a
chili supper, vacation bible school
or mission trip.

❑ Photo of you at your baptism/bat
mitzvah.

❑ Photo of you taken around the
same time as a spiritual "epipha-
ny" or discovery.

Ideas for memorabilia

❑ Prayer cloth or rosary.

❑ Bulletin from a worship service.

❑ Your minister's calling card.

❑ Scan of blueprints from a religious
building expansion.

❑ Color copy or scan of your favorite
song from a hymnal.

❑ Color copy or scan of your favorite
verse from a scripture.

❑ Soil from the Holy Land (stored in
a memorabilia pocket).

A Friend Loves at All Times
by Toni Patton

This layout commemorates
the many friends Toni has
made while working at her
church. It includes what
she admires about each
person and how blessed
she feels to spend time
with them.

Note the technique Toni
used to mat a special
photo. She stamped on vellum and embossed it, then
placed it behind the photo.
Then, she tore a hole out
of a rectangle of cardstock
and curled the torn edges a
little. She placed the torn-
hole mat over the picture
and vellum, then matted
the whole thing on cream
cardstock.

SUPPLIES: Stamp by Stampin'
Up!

A Journey in FAITH

This is the prayer cloth. Mama put a label on it that said, "Vicki With Love from The Trinity Family." I touched it so much that the words are about worn off!

God was so merciful to confirm His care for us. Three different times He sent confirmation that He was in control. I wrote them on post-it notes and kept them on my computer at work.

1 There was a message given during the prayer over the prayer cloth. The main thought of it was, "I am the giver of life. I have it all in control."

2 My long-lost friend Dar sent me an e-mail with the verse that her daughter was learning - "Fear not; for I am with thee." Isaiah 43:5

3 One morning shortly after we had seen the baby's heartbeat during an ultrasound, I woke up singing "Joy in the Camp." Then I heard God's voice (and He was chuckling!). He said, "And you thought I wasn't listening!"

Fear not; for I am with thee. Is 43:5

"I am the giver of life. I have it all in control" 10/5/1997

"And you thought I wasn't listening!"

THINKING OF YOU And you thought I wasn't Listening

Jerry and I had been trying to have a baby since May 1996. (I quit drinking Diet Cokes on May 19, 1996. My family and close friends will know that was an indicator that I was serious - I was a true Diet Coke addict!) We did conceive but sadly, lost that baby to miscarriage in April 1997 (the same week we learned that Grandma Thomas had cancer).

This was very difficult to understand. I had prayed every night for that baby and now I was losing it. When I got home from the doctor's office I sat on the end of the bed and cried out to God. I told Him exactly how I felt. I told Him, "God, I know you're out there but I don't feel like you're listening. I feel like you've abandoned me. But still, I trust you."

It took us awhile to conceive again. When I was truly able to give my doubts, fears, longings - everything, to God, it happened. On September 30, 1997 we had a positive pregnancy test.

That same morning the enemy came in like a roaring, I become very fearful that we might lose this baby, too. I had trouble sleeping and cried a lot. Poor Jerry! He hardly knew what to do with me. But he was wonderful. He was always ready with a hug or a smile or to just hold me and let me cry. He also covered me with prayer. Still, I kept my confession of faith, "God, I may not feel like you're listening but I trust You!"

In the midst of my fear, God confirmed his love over and over that He was there.

One day, Dar Ridley, a college friend, was writing an email to me when her daughter gave her the memory verse for the week. "This is incredible, Vicki. This verse is for you," she wrote. "Fear not; for I am with you." (Isaiah 43:5) That word was like water

on parched ground. And it began to crack the wall of doubt and fear. "I trust you, God!" I wrote that verse on a sticky note and put it on my computer at work as a constant reminder of God's faithfulness.

During a particularly difficult day, I called Daddy (pastor of our church in Oklahoma). We believe that prayer cloths can be anointed as a symbol of our faith and prayer. I asked him to have the church send me a prayer cloth and they did. Mama told me about a message that had been given over the prayer cloth by Billy Gene Wesson on October 5, 1997. Basically, it was that God said, "I am the giver of life. I have it all in control." (I wrote that on a sticky note and put it on the computer, too.) For months I kept that cloth pinned to the inside of my clothes. When I felt fearful I'd touch the cloth as a reminder that there were many people praying for us. I would continually say, "I trust You, God!"

We saw the baby's heartbeat during an ultrasound on October 21, 1997. What a relief and a joy! I was feeling so much more confident and still making my confession of faith, "I trust You, God!"

One morning shortly after the ultrasound, I woke up singing a song from the Bill Gaither video, Joy in the Camp. God spoke to me (and He was chuckling!). He said, "And you thought I wasn't listening!" Jerry sent me flowers that day and on the card he wrote, "And you thought I wasn't listening!"

What an amazing journey through faith this pregnancy was! I don't know why we lost our first baby. I don't know why it sometimes feels like God doesn't hear us when we pray. I do know that God is faithful and that I will trust Him!

Journey of Faith
by Vicki Owens

The power of this layout comes from the memorabilia and journaling. Vicki included the actual prayer cloth that saw her through a trying time. She added the Post-it Notes that contained the comforting Bible verses. Her journaling is detailed and includes many of her intimate concerns and thoughts during her pregnancy. The result is a testimony to a faith journey and the great leaps of faith she made during this time.

SUPPLIES: Paper is Green Leaf Paper by Colors by Design. Cardstock is by Bazzill Basics. Stencil is Block Upper Case, ABC Traces by EK Success. Font is CK Cursive by Creating Keepsakes.

STANDING ON THE ROCK

So what are you waiting for? Get up and get yourself baptized, scrubbed clean of those sins and personally acquainted with God
Acts 22:16
The Message Bible

Reading my personal testimony at church. Joe and Wesley were in the front row watching and taking pictures of this very important moment.

Daybreak community

I was baptized the first time in 1988 shortly after Joe and I were married. I was a relatively new Christian and Pastor Wright at KC First Church of the Nazarene was so excited to baptize one of it's newest members. However, I wasn't entirely sure what it all meant. Not wanting to disappoint the excitement that everyone felt about my pending baptism I went ahead and was baptized.

Fast forward to 2001 and to Daybreak Community Church. Joe and I joined this church after much searching for a new church home. We fell totally in love with it's pastor, Steve Reed. He announced in early summer that he was having a baptism service on July 11th and those who wish to be baptized would give their testimony at church then everyone would go to Shawnee Mission Park for the actual baptism. Being baptized at SM Park was very special because it was a place that held many fond memories for me growing up. I wanted to be baptized at this time because of the TREMENDOUS changes in my walk with the Lord since I was first married. I felt now that being baptized would now include feelings in my heart and not just my head. What was so special was Wesley was here and able to witness this and hear my testimony.

The response from the church members was overwhelming. Many came to me and said my testimony was their testimony. The pastor said many were touched by my story. It continues to amaze me that anything I could say would be meaningful to anyone else. Because of my testimony I have been able to meet and bond with my new church family and feel I have found my true church home. I have been truly blessed!

Carol Hughes October 2001

Above: Pastor Steve Reed asks me if I have accepted Jesus Christ as my personal Savior.

Below: I have been REBORN and came up out of the water with such joy for Jesus!

MY ACTUAL PERSONAL TESTIMONY

Standing on the Rock *by Carol Hughes*

This layout honors Carol's journey toward becoming a baptized Christian and how much the experience meant to her. For memorabilia, she included the actual notes from which she gave her testimony the day she was baptized as well as the logo from the church website.

SUPPLIES: Vellum is by Paper Garden. Lettering template is Fat Caps by Frances Meyer. Eyelets are by Coffee Break Designs. Jute is by Westrim. Chalk is by Craf-T Products. Font is CK Journaling by Creating Keepsakes.

15: ALL ABOUT ME

Definition of this role:

This role allows you to showcase all the things that are absolutely unique to you. Here you can identify and display your favorite things and pastimes, what makes you happy, and all the other things that make you YOU.

The "All About Me" section provides a space for your "happy thoughts"—the things that you like simply because YOU like them.

Ask yourself how your friends or children might describe you. I often jokingly tell my son, "There's two things I like about chocolate cake: It's chocolate and it's cake." He always laughs when we share that little joke, because if there's one thing he knows about his Mama, it's that she loves chocolate!

What do other people know about you? If someone else would describe you and how you spend your time, what would they pick out as definitive about you? Create layouts about those things! These are the things that your family and friends will look back on and smile, and nod, because they define you as unique.

Your tastes and interests distinguish you from others. The things that you love, the things that make you smile, are as individual as snowflakes—all your interests and tastes combined together will result only in YOU. You are the only person through all of time that has this exact combination of favorites. What do your unique likes and dislikes say about you? What kind of person are you?

In my scrapbook...

I created a page on my favorite food, colors and singers. I did layouts on the "Top Ten Ways to Make My Day" and the "Top Ten Things I Like About Me." I also included a layout of my favorite quotes and why they appeal to me.

Favorite Things
by Kerri Sox

Kerri made up this poem to the rhythm of the song "My Favorite things" from "The Sound of Music." She thought it would be a good introduction for her hobby scrapbook.

SUPPLIES: Patterned paper by Kangaroo & Joey. Cardstock by Making Memories. Wire by Wild Wire. Eyelets by Impress Rubber Stamps. Font is Scubadoo downloaded from fontfreak.com.

Baskets and family and music and cooking. Traveling, laughing, and lots of scrapbooking. Gardens and Moss prints and when my dad sings—

These are a few of my *Favorite things*

Kerri Beth Sox
August 2001

Prompts to trigger journaling

❏ What are your favorites?:

 o I love the color... It reminds me of...

 o Foods: are you a carnivore or an herbivore? Do you prefer meat and potatoes or pasta primavera?

 o Restaurants

 o Songs, bands and composers

 o Movie(s)

 o Poems and quotes

❏ Hobbies or interests—when and why did you start?

❏ What brings you joy? Make a list of your "happy thoughts."

❏ What does your name mean? Do you think it's accurate? What name would you choose for yourself? Why? Make a name poem using the letters of your name (see the websites listed on page 76 for how to write the ABC's of your name and how to find out the meaning of your name).

❏ Complete this sentence: I am good at...

❏ What makes you laugh?

❏ What books or movies have influenced you? How?

❏ What is your favorite musical or play? What do you like about that production?

❏ How do you relax? What do you find comforting?

❏ Where do you go to find inspiration?

Self-love is the source of all our other loves.
 —Pierre Corneille

Nothing can bring you peace but yourself.
 —Ralph Waldo Emerson

Resolve to be thyself; and know, that he who finds himself, loses his misery.
 —Matthew Arnold

Oh watch me go
I'm a happy girl, everybody knows
That the sweetest thing that you'll ever see
In the whole wide world is a happy girl
 —"Happy Girl" sung by Martina McBride

A strong woman won't let anyone get the best of her ... but a woman of strength gives the best of her to everyone.
 —Unknown

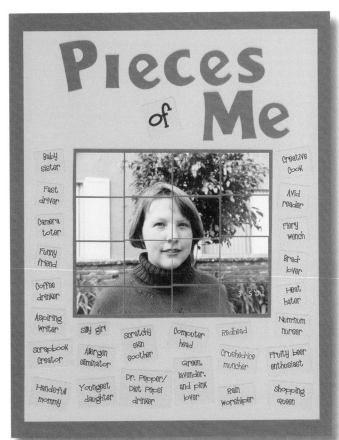

Pieces of Me
by Jennifer Wohlenberg

This layout is a cornerstone of the Book of Me concept. All of the pieces are varied and seemingly miscellaneous but add up to equal her whole self. (Jennifer cut the photograph into uneven pieces deliberately to symbolize that not all of our pieces are equally sized.) A similar layout could be done to represent various points of your life—childhood, your wedding day, the birth of a child, or another big event. It would be interesting to see how the "pieces" of you change (or, perhaps, don't change) from event to event.

SUPPLIES: Lettering template is Kiki from Scrap Pagerz. Font is Mandingo.

I've lived a life that's full.
I've traveled each and ev'ry
highway;
But more, much more than
this,
I did it my way.
    —P. Anka/C. Francois
    J. Reyaux/G. Thibault

You are beautiful beyond de-
scription
Too marvelous for words
Too wonderful for compre-
hension
Like nothing ever seen or
heard
Who can grasp your infinite
wisdom
Who can fathom the depths
of your love
You are beautiful beyond de-
scription
Majesty enthroned above
    —Unknown

Do you know what you are?
You are a marvel. You are
unique.
In all the years that have
passed, there has never been
another child like you.
Your legs, your arms, your
clever fingers, the way you
move.
You may become a Shake-
speare, a Michelangelo, a
Beethoven.
You have the capacity for
anything.
    —Pablo Casals

I am Special
Hundreds of birds in the sky,
Hundreds of fish in the sea,
Hundreds of flowers in the
field
But there's only one of me!
    —Unknown

- Talk about what success means to you.
- What has sustained your soul?
- What is the meaning of life to you?
- Create a list: The 20 most important things to do with my life.
- Create another list: Likes and dislikes.
- What are your pet peeves?
- Create a page based on this thought: There is so much within me that is beautiful...(Get outside input on this one, if need be.)
- I want to be remembered for...
- What are your favorite qualities about yourself? You could make this a top ten list, or you could write about them in paragraph form. Consider including diction-ary definitions about these qualities or using a thesaurus to look up other descriptive terms.

Photo opportunities

- A picture of you wearing your favorite outfit or your favorite color.
- A picture of you engaged in your hobby of choice.
- A picture of you laughing.
- A picture of you in your comfiest clothes, or just relaxing.
- A picture of your favorite spot to relax—a comfy chair, a lake cottage or the mountains.
- A photo of your favorite recipe, prepared.
- A photo of your favorite candles.
- A photo of anything you collect.

Things I Love
by Kayla Schwisow

Kayla is a teen scrapper and she loves scrapbook-ing her life and seeing how the things she loves change over time. But, she notes, some things won't ever change.

SUPPLIES: Diecut hearts and frame by O'Scraps.

Ideas for memorabilia

- ❑ Color copy or scan of sheet music to your favorite song or just the lyrics (you can print them from the Internet).
- ❑ The recipe for your favorite comfort food.
- ❑ Program to your favorite play, musical or music concert.
- ❑ Menu from your favorite restaurant.
- ❑ Color copy or scan of the label from your favorite perfume or body lotion.
- ❑ Color copy or scan of your favorite album or CD cover, or video jacket for your favorite movie.

Right Now *by Shimelle Laine*

This is the closing page of Shimelle's album, "Life…So Far." It is not a monumental event, it's just where she was when she made this album. Shimelle can pick up there when she decides to add more to her story.

SUPPLIES: Patterned paper is Burgundy Swirl by Crafter's Workshop. Stickers are: birthday present by Frances Meyer, school house by Susan Branch for Colorbok, globe and cups by Debbie Mumm for Creative Imaginations, dance shoes by Neena Chawa for Creative Imaginations, cat by Hot Off the Press and camera by SRM Press. Chalk is by Craf-T Products. Lettering is Breeze from Creating Keepsakes. Photo is by Jane Dean.

I am the only unique me that will ever be. I have the power to make a difference in this world.
I look forward to taking on the grand adventure of life, living, and always remembering to be myself… I love being me!
—Unknown

I was born to catch dragons in their dens
And pick flowers
To tell tales and laugh away the morning
To drift and dream like a lazy stream
And walk barefoot across sunshine days.
—James Kavanaugh

May the child within your heart stay forever.
—Unknown

There's something joyful and comforting about ice cream.
—Unknown

A good time for laughing is when you can.
—Unknown

My therapist told me the way to achieve true inner peace is to finish what I start. So far today, I have finished two bags of chips and a Chocolate cake. I feel better already.
—Unknown

WWW.

Create a Happy Book:
www.writersdigest.com/
journaling/articles/
0801happy.asp

www.desktopworks.com/
happy.htm

www.writingthejourney.com/
exercises/happylist.htm

Growing Myself article:
www.positiveperfectyou.com/
article1012.html

Writing about your favorite
song(s):
www.inspired2write.com/
wordweav/exers/
yoursong.html

Find lyrics to songs:
lyrics.astraweb.com/

Write the ABC's of your
name:
www.inspired2write.com/
wordweav/exers/
warmabc.html

Use the alphabet to de-
scribe yourself:
www.inspired2write.com/
wordweav/exers/
warmalph.html

Define your personal skills,
talents and core qualities:
www.angelfire.com/journal/
inspirare/julysoul.html

The meaning of your name:
www.namestusa.com/
index.html

Top names by decade:
www.behindthename.com/
top.html

Top 10 Ways to Make My Day
by Angie Pedersen

I compiled this list pretty quickly, just thinking about things that other people did for me that made me happy. Ice cream (#7) is a big thing for me, so I included the cute gift card by Susan Branch as well as a photo of me eating ice cream. I also printed out a complimentary e-mail I received on my web-site to illustrate #2 on my list. The design of the back-ground paper is really strong so I matted each element on the layout to make it stand out from the background.

SUPPLIES: : Patterned paper is by Colors by Design. Cardstock is by Crafter's Workshop. Diecut is by Susan Branch. Title font is CK Flair, Wedding Alphabets by Creating Keepsakes; journaling font is Joplin by Bright Ideas.

Top 10 Things I Like About Me!
by Angie Pedersen

Several people said to me that they couldn't come up with 10 "whole" things that they liked about themselves. To create this list, I just listened to my conversations and e-mails with other people. If someone compliment-ed me on something and I thought, "Yeah. I like that about me, too", then it went on my list. So basically, I just sat back and waited for people to say nice things about me! Once I had a few things contributed by others, I was able to finish the list on my own. Try it—you might be surprised.

SUPPLIES: Patterned paper is by Colors by Design. Cardstock is by Crafter's Workshop. Title font is CK Flair, Wedding Alphabets by Creating Keepsakes; journaling font is Joplin by Bright Ideas

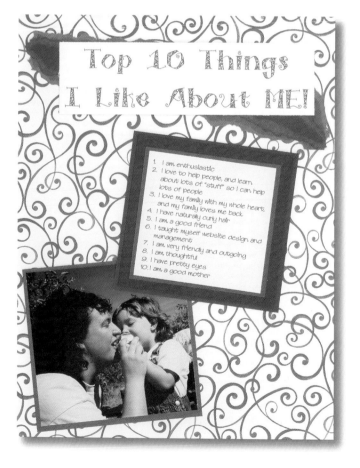

A Few More Tips

Here are a few final tips for creating your Book of Me:

❑ Get some note paper. Set aside a block of time for a brainstorming session. Plan to enjoy your memories!

❑ Make a list of the roles you fill in your life. A role is often a familial connection, like mother, sister, daughter, wife, or it tells us how you spend your time—your job description, hobbies and social activities.

❑ Some of your roles may match ones I've provided in the chapters of this book, and some may not. That's what makes this project so personal—it can be tailored to your life!

❑ Pick a role and read through the prompts. Jot down images and memories that come to mind.

❑ Write out all your answers (handwritten or typed) before putting together your layouts. Don't censor your thoughts here—just jot it all down. Think of this as a working draft.

❑ Once everything is written, look through your photos and memorabilia. What can you use to support what you want to say? Remember, photos don't have to be of a particular event—a photo of you taken around that same time is great. Decide what you want to say first, then find photos to "prove" your point.

❑ Gather your written material and your supporting evidence. Work on one layout at a time.

❑ Take some time to look over the quotes offered in each section. Consider using a quote as the basis for a layout. Choose a quote that "speaks" to you and journal about why it moves you.

Organizing your materials

Once you have your list of roles and a general idea of the roles you'd like to highlight, create a "home" for all your materials.

Keep tabs on your ideas by using a creativity notebook along with these ideas from Shimelle Laine, member of both Creating Keepsakes' Hallx of Fame and PaperKuts Power Team. Shimelle uses a spiral bound notebook with white pages for her ideas. She started a new one just for her Book of Me.

Shimelle divides her notebooks into sections. Some of her sections include page topics, layout sketches, quotes and stories. Her most important section, however, is the "things I want to find" section. Here, she keeps a list of photos and memorabilia that she wants to include on a page, but doesn't have on hand and needs to ask friends and family for.

If you want to keep your notes in a spiral bound notebook, look for a five-subject notebook with pocket dividers for each section. Use the pockets for storing the memorabilia related to each role. Or, use a three-ring binder for your ideas and add three-hole punched pocket dividers.

The key is to keep all your notes, ideas, and memorabilia in one central location so you know right where to find everything.

Organizational Note:

I used a three-ring binder to keep all my material together as I was writing this book. I bought 16 dividers, and used one for each chapter. I kept a blank notebook paper in each section so I could jot down any quotes or ideas I found.

Resources to Help You Begin Scrapbooking:

Let's Start Scrapbooking at One Scrappy Site!:
www.onescrappysite.com/beginners.htm

Graceful Bee's Guide for NewBees:
www.gracefulbee.com/newbees/index.html

Graceful Bee's glossary of scrapbooking terms:
www.gracefulbee.com/glossary.html

Back to Basics with Scrapbooking.com:
scrapbooking.com/2000/2000/07/head_of_the_class/class01.htm

To locate a Creative Memories consultant near you for an in-home class:
www.creativememories.com/locatecnslt.asp

To locate a Close to My Heart consultant near you for an in-home class:
www.closetomyheart.com/ (Click on "Find a Consultant.")

To find a scrapbooking store near you that may offer beginner's classes:
www.creatingkeepsakes.com/letsscrapbook/locator/

Few or no photos?

I frequently hear, "I don't have good pictures of myself." My response? Go take them now! Film costs $3 a roll plus $6 for processing... that's $9. For 24 pictures of yourself, it's worth it!

For childhood photos, take heart. Some of the best layouts have no photos. They are the ones with an entire page devoted to journaling, artistically displayed with some card-stock accents. The key is to paint your memories with words.

Painting a scene with words

Use this formula:

1. The setting is your canvas. Where does your story take place? Your home? A restaurant? Your school? What does the room or the landscape look like? Describe the furnishings, decorations or any landmarks.

2. Use your senses. What do you hear in this place? What do you see? Turn around 360 degrees and describe what is behind you, to the side, above you, and below you. Who is with you? What do you taste? What do you feel? Is it warm or cool in this place? Is anything slick, hard, soft, fuzzy? Do you associate any fabrics with this place or event?

3. A good story has a plot. What action is taking place? What's the background of the story? Why are these people gathered together? How often do they get together? What's the most exciting thing that happened on this occasion? What's the "climax" of the story? What happened afterward?

4. Bring it on home. Offer insight gained by hindsight. What was the best thing about that time, event or place? What didn't you like? What did you admire about the people involved? What did you learn by participating? How did it affect you?

Decorate it

Add visual elements to your journaling-driven layouts. For example, say you spend a day at the beach and a crab crawls in your husband's swim trunks. You want to preserve the memory of your husband dancing around trying to gingerly dislodge the crab but you have no photos. Think of the "ingredients" of the story that could serve as decorative elements: crab, swimsuit, sand, ocean, water, sunshine, husband. You could:

❑ Go back to the beach and take photos of where the event took place, or road signs pointing to that particular beach.

❑ Use photos of the beach, or your husband in his swimming suit, that you already have developed, but not necessarily taken at the same time and place as the "crab-in-swimsuit" incident.

❑ Use a crab diecut and make a border using cardstock torn to look like sand to decorate your page.

❑ Get some sand and shells and put them in a memorabilia pocket to include on your page.

❑ Take a photo of your husband eating crab at home or at a restaurant, then journal about how that makes you "remember that one time at the beach..."

We often create layouts based on fabulous pictures that make us smile. The photos make the entire layout. But sometimes the photos just aren't there; sometimes we just have the memories. Make pages about those precious memories anyway! The stories are all there... just waiting for you to paint the picture.

INDEX

Go ahead... Make Angie's Day! *(see page 76).*

Visit Angie online at www.scrapyourstories.com:

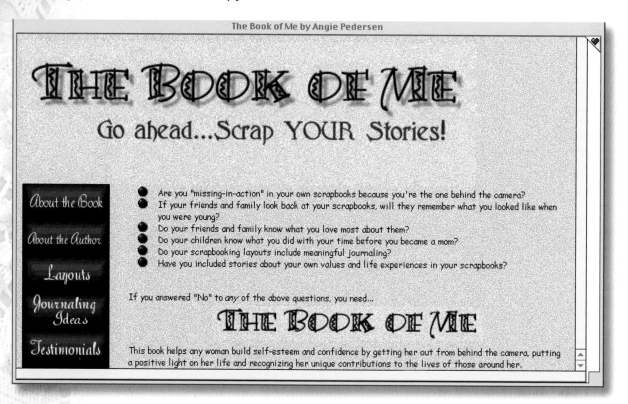

Click on the "mailing list" button and sign up to join other scrapbookers who are making their "Books of Me" at www.scrapyourstories.com/maillist.htm: